American Society for Training and Development

Distance Learning

A Step-by-Step Guide for Trainers

› Select the best technologies

› Explore implementation strategies

› Integrate DL into your training program

By Karen Mantyla and J. Richard Gividen

Ordering information: Books published by the American Society for Training and Development can be ordered by calling 703/683-8100.

Library of Congress Catalog Card Number: 97-071602
ISBN: 1-56286-060-7

We're glad you have this book, as it is an investment in your future success. You've chosen a career as a training professional or have been given responsibilities to train others. We want to help ensure your success as a 21st-century trainer and welcome you to the exciting world of distance learning.

Our primary audience for this book are those involved in the management and delivery of traditional on-site training. Whether through self-directed initiatives or a corporate mandate, you want and need to find new ways to train your workforce. You are tasked with either converting selected existing classroom instruction to a distance learning format or developing training that will be delivered by one or more distance learning technologies. You need to do it, and this book can help you get started.

Imagine that you are looking for new career opportunities. You see an ad in the paper, and the only reference is to a World Wide Web page on the Internet. You check it out, and here's what you find. (See the illustration at right.)

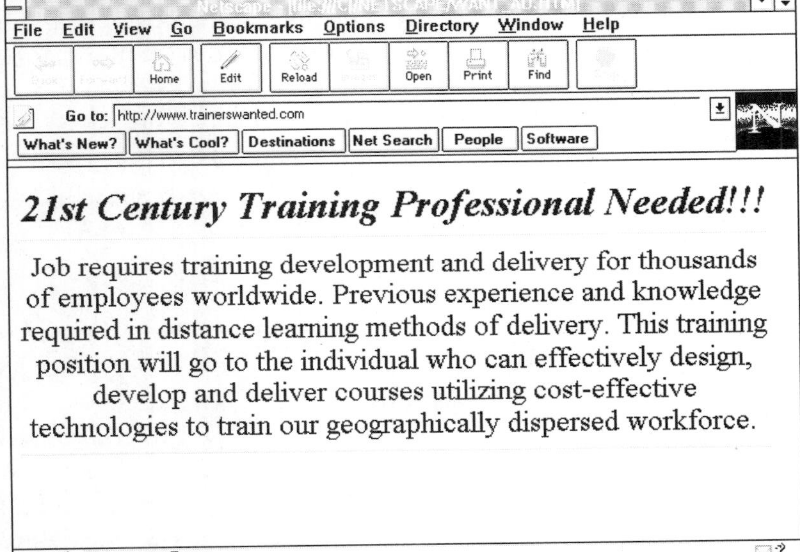

Fact or fiction? It won't be very long before a distance learning experience will be a prerequisite to consideration for training positions in the 21st century.

Our goal is to provide you with a step-by-step guide for understanding and delivering training utilizing distance learning methods of delivery. This book is not written for "techies." It is written by and for training professionals who know what they want to achieve: effective learning outcomes and skill development and enhancement for all learners. We are not technology experts, but we have learned to become experts about which technologies can best be utilized for desired training environments and outcomes. We also have learned what we need to know and what we need to do to achieve success in this new learner-centered virtual training environment. It's a new world and as training professionals, we must be learners ourselves to achieve success for the people we train.

We will, often reluctantly, give up old mindsets to learn new ways of thinking. The new mindset is not focused on what can I teach, but on how can I help facilitate the learning for learners? The trainers that will be most successful will be those who quickly adapt to this new mindset. These leading-edge thinkers will uncover ways to deliver education and training when and where the learners want and need it. They will design learner-centered guidance systems that will enhance learners' critical thinking skills while helping them absorb and understand learning content. That's the new bottom line and cash in the bank for your future.

Our learning environment is changing faster than at anytime in history. We know that you want to have as many options as possible to address the ongoing needs and priorities of both your internal and external customers. And you want your customers to want and need more of your training expertise.

We will achieve these results by utilizing different methods of training delivery: on site (we don't have to give this up, as we'll discuss later) and via distance learning training options. There are numerous distance learning technologies to choose from, and we cite today's most widely used live, interactive technologies (as opposed to self-paced instructional technologies). These examples will illustrate the process of how to integrate these distance learning options and strategies into your training programs.

Mention distance learning to training professionals, and you'll hear some or all of these statements:

"It won't work as well as on-site training."
"I don't know anything about the technology and don't want to look stupid."
"They won't learn as much."
"I don't know where to start."
"I've seen demonstrations of incredible products—the technology is great!"
"I like to travel, and so do the participants."
"They won't need me."
"Training is or will be outsourced."
"I don't have time to do this."
"My workload is already stressful."
"It will take too long to learn."
"I can't do it."

Have any of these thoughts entered your mind? They sure did for us. As 15-year veteran trainers, we were skeptical about many key issues. For many years, we only taught on site. We had lots of doubts in the beginning, yet challenges of time, cost, and geography forced us to look at alternative methods of delivery, not just one "it feels good and I already know how to do it" method.

We tried distance learning, had a few failures along the way, and then learned how to succeed. Now we would never go back to using only one method of delivery. This book is designed to provide you with a step-by-step focus on the key areas that will help you achieve success in distance learning initiatives and results. It is not intended to provide you with every detail for every aspect of distance learning. Many trainers who apply the practices and principles recommended here will save between six and 12 months of effort in implementing their own distance learning program.

There are resources available that focus on only one type of technology, on one aspect of distance learning, or on a theoretical perspective that will cause you to think about your own learning environment. We want you to search out and get fine-tuned details on the elements that are most important to you. As such, we have included an appendix listing resources to help guide you to any additional and specific information that you want or need.

Our goal for you, our reader, is to share with you what we have learned along the way about distance learning, how we continuously keep learning, and how to succeed as a 21st-century trainer. With technology changing at such a rapid pace and a dizzying array of information available from an infinite number of sources, our goal is to provide you with a rock-solid foundation of where to start, what to do, and where to go for help. Technologies and their related costs are changing every day. That is a constant and is a part of our training world. Keeping up with the changing technologies will allow greater flexibility and options as we strengthen our professional expertise as distance learning professionals.

This will be your base upon which to build your future, as you desire it to be. Welcome to an exciting world of distance learning opportunities...with technology solutions as your partner in effectively training your 21st-century workforce.

Karen Mantyla **J. Richard Gividen**

Beginning Your Distance Learning Journey

Every road leads somewhere. Or at least it should. Like every skilled navigator, you decide what you want and where you want to go, find out how to get there, calculate how to reach your final destination, and target checkpoints to be sure you've reached the right place.

We recognize that we must find more effective ways to train a geographically dispersed workforce, analyze what we need to do and why we need to do it, select a solution, implement that solution, and evaluate our results. We also realize that we must find ways to reduce the costs associated with this training. With your interest in distance learning and with this book as a guide to help you toward a successful journey, you can find a way to do both. Using the components of a generic instructional systems design (ISD) model will help you take it a step at a time. A systems approach is extremely important because looking at distance learning options and opportunities as a whole can be overwhelming and result in information overload. Each of you has different training challenges and needs for your workforce and must select specific training solutions based on your current and anticipated priorities.

The saying "walk a mile in my shoes" paints a picture of how we designed the sections, chapter headings, and content for you. We decided to design the flow in the way we wish we could have learned. It would have made our entry into the world of distance learning easier if we knew where to start, how to progress, what to look for (and look out for), and ways to help ensure training success. By putting ourselves at the beginning of our distance learning journey, we have structured the book in a step-by-step fashion to help you pinpoint what you want to know now. You may be starting at the beginning of your distance learning journey or have the experience of being a seasoned distance learning trainer. For learners at both ends of the spectrum, we have provided various checklists throughout the book to help cover all the key bases for continuous distance learning success. We've included a Distance Learning Master Plan Checklist at the end of this section to help ensure that no steps in your journey will be missed as well as a Distance Learning Failure Factors checklist indicating some of those risks. We will share lessons learned and mistakes that have been made so that you can learn from them and be proactive and start off right.

Our initial thoughts as we started writing this book included, "What's in it for me?" A natural question and one we want to address early on in the book. You've chosen a career as a training professional, and you want to be successful. We know the one constant in business is change. So we can't stand still using *only* the one tried-and-true method we know: on-site training. The workplace environment, needs of the learners, increased competition, reduced budgets, increased need for technical skills, and the consistent need for mandated, functional, and soft skills training and retraining are keeping us out of breath. Yet, we need to deliver cost-effective, high-quality ongoing training. An impossible task? No, but we can't achieve it all with on-site training. On-site training is not going to disappear in its entirety. It is simply going to be one way, but not the only way, to deliver training to the learners at the office, at home, and on the road. We need to find new ways and new solutions to our training challenges. The 21st-century trainers will learn what they need to do and how to do it. Distance learning options will help provide solutions to training needs and requirements. We now will start at the beginning.

Chapter One

What Is Distance Learning?

Introduction

What is distance learning? It seems like an easy enough question, right? Karen Mantyla was attending a major annual conference on human resource management two years ago, and the director of training for a Fortune 500 corporation was sitting next to her. The keynote speaker touched on the need to reach the workforce in new and creative ways: "Distance learning is the way to go." The speaker then moved on to another point, and the director of training leaned over to Karen and said, "Right…distance learning is the way to go, but who knows where to start? My phone rings constantly from vendors who say they have the best distance learning equipment. Razzle dazzle technology. Equipment for what? Somehow, I think other things should come first, but I'm not quite sure what they are. Besides, what exactly is distance learning?"

That director of training is not alone. Ask five people the definition of distance learning, and you will often get five different answers. The reason is that there is so much information being disseminated on the subject and its related technologies, plus it is constantly changing. When we have asked participants in our workshops to define distance learning, we have been given answers such as

"It's the Internet."
"It's using technology to deliver training."
"It's computer-based training."
"It's using satellites."
"It's using an Intranet."
"It's virtual reality."
"It's video teleconferencing."
"It's audio teleconferencing."

Distance learning is all of the above and more. If you try to start your distance learning journey with this list, it can be overwhelming. The list is not the best place to start.

"Distance learning" is an umbrella term that covers many different ways to deliver training, including methods not yet delivered. This variety allows you to select the appropriate method of delivering distance learning to suit your ever-changing needs and requirements.

Definition of Distance Learning

The following definition is from the "Guiding Principles for Distance Learning in a Learning Society," by the Center for Adult Learning and Educational Credentials of the American Council on Education.

Distance learning is a system and a process that connects learners with distributed learning resources. While distance learning takes a wide variety of forms, all distance learning is characterized by:

- separation of place and/or time between instructor and learner, among learners, and/or between learners and learning resources

- interaction between the learner and the instructor, among learners and/or between learners and learning resources conducted through one or more media; use of electronic media is not necessarily required.

The learner is an individual or group that seeks a learning experience offered by a provider. The provider is the organization that creates and facilitates the learning opportunity. The provider approves and monitors the quality of the learning experience. Providers include schools, colleges and universities, business and industry, professional organizations, labor unions, government agencies, the military and other public and private organizations.

Another definition you may hear is that "distance learning" is any learning that takes place without the physical presence of the instructor with the learner. Note that these definitions don't mean you have to use technology or electronic media, a point illuminated by the American Council on Education: Correspondence courses, a distance learning method utilizing print-based programs, have been around for a long time.

These definitions embrace the wide range of opportunities to select the best way or ways to reach learners depending on

- training needs assessment outcomes
- learner needs
- organizational needs
- course requirements
- trainer needs
- environmental needs and requirements.

We will use the term "learners" throughout the book to help position the fact that to be truly successful, distance learning systems and decisions about those systems must always revolve around the needs of the learners. This focus on the learners is somewhat of a mindset shift for many trainers, and a mindset that must shift if the trainer and distance learning team wants to succeed. We cannot overstate this point enough, and we want to emphasize this very early in the book.

Karen conducted an introductory workshop on distance learning for veteran trainers (10 plus years experience) and instructional designers. She asked the participants to tell her their first thoughts when they heard the words "distance learning." Here's a list of their responses:

"There goes my job."
"I'll look 10 pounds heavier on TV."

"Lack of classroom control."
"Talking head."
"You have to stay put—can't roam."
"No more travel—I like to travel."
"I like the physical presence of students."
"It won't be effective."
"Boring."
"Lack of interaction responses and responsiveness."
"It's like a Broadway show."
"Impersonal."
"I'd rather have liposuction!"

These are natural thoughts, yes, and we hear them quite often. The main reason for listing these comments is that they are from the perspective of the trainer. But now it's a new mindset. We must look at the training and education needs from the perspective of the learner. That's the mindset foundation needed by every successful distance learning trainer.

Why Use Distance Learning?

The training needs of your workforce will automatically convert into the training needs of your organization. In a white paper, G. Kevin Lane targets bottom-line answers that the AT&T Center for Excellence in Distance Learning (CEDL) gave to the question, "Why use distance learning?" CEDL also identified those reasons, which follow, as the potential training problems that senior management faces when trying to shape its business:

- the need to increase global competitiveness
- ensuring that the workforce keeps up with and implements rapidly changing technology
- coping with major changes in the nature of the workforce. These major changes require frequent skill updates, skill development, and training in how to cope with the information glut and rapidly changing needs and priorities.

Benefits of Distance Learning

Thousands of universities, hundreds of corporations, and government agencies all have experienced the benefits of distance learning, which include the following:

Cost-Effectiveness

More people can be trained more often with different distance learning tools. Travel costs can be reduced and productivity increased because no time is lost from travel to on-site training. Subject matter experts can be brought in without leaving their hometowns.

Quality of Instruction

Learners can have access to more resources, which adds to their body of knowledge in any given topic.

In an article, Hank Payne, program manager of distance learning, Federal Aviation Administration (FAA), and Robbie Smith, senior training program specialist, Department of Energy (DOE), discuss the "significant reductions in student training time and costs." The federal government, through the consortium called GATE (Government Alliance for Training and Education), has documented research showing the cost-savings elements of distance learning. In all sectors, public and private, budget cuts and reductions in workforce are helping to stimulate the increased use of distance learning.

Distance Learning Effectiveness

One of the statements many trainers make is that they are concerned about the effectiveness of distance learning training. The fact is that those organizations that use distance learning have documented proof that it works. In Appendix B of this book, we list many organizations that use distance learning and have documented its effectiveness as well as people you can speak with at those organizations. This information should be not only reassuring to you as a dedicated training professional, but it should also be valuable when you need to justify dollars invested in distance learning delivery systems. Others have proved that distance learning is a cost-effective, profitable solution to meet training requirements.

According to a Pennsylvania State University report of 1992, distance learning is equal to or superior to learning in the traditional classroom. This view is supported by both private- and public-sector organizations like UNISYS, the U.S. Department of Defense, FORD, AT&T, and the University of Wisconsin that are following the effectiveness of their distance learning initiatives. All of these organizations are continuing to provide funding for distance learning training tools. Money is approved only when it is justified as profitable to the organization, and continuing funding means it's working. That's the bottom line.

Major Trends in Distance Learning

There are major trends emerging:

Competitive Strategy

The trends show that organizations are using distance learning as a competitive strategy. These organizations include educational institutions that must compete with others in their hometown and around the world (distance learning brings learning right to the learners' personal computer [PC]) as well as public- and private-sector organizations. Corporations are using public resources to enhance their ability to serve their internal and external customers. Federal agencies are being privatized and using commercial and educational providers. Educational institutions are using all sectors. In the age of competition, joint alliances and partnerships for training and education will continue to grow.

The amount of information and speed of information transmittal necessary to effectively arm today's workforce with needed facts and skills requires using different types of technologies. Reaching geographically dispersed workers and specialists is a must. Technologies developed for distance learning are being introduced and addressed as not just "nice to have," but also as "must have" in some fashion or another.

Organizations like UNISYS started their distance learning network based on marketing wants and needs. COMP USA uses its network for product introductions and communications as well as training. How can you get a competitive edge with your customers? Reach a lot of them faster than anyone else. How can you address ongoing product introductions and information to your sales team (giving them a jump-start on the competition)? Distance learning provides a link to make it happen. Time-sensitive training and information can be communicated around the world in a consistent fashion. Everyone can hear the same information without variations on the content, and they can electronically collaborate with their colleagues and participate in discussing powerful solutions and application possibilities that can fuel growth for the organization.

Self-Directed Learning Initiatives

Workers are realizing that many skills they develop today will not only enhance their current job, but also support the success of their opportunities for career and personal development. They often change jobs and redirect work goals, and their future challenge becomes self-directed: What do I want to learn? What do I need to learn? What skills will help me now or later?

The worker is then in the driver's seat to find ways, tools, and courses that will provide the foundation for self-directed learning. This learning can take place anywhere—on the job, on the road, or at home. Whether by computer, audio, video, print, or satellite, all types of training are available for today's workforce. Trainers simply can't afford to provide only the option of traditional—classroom—training delivery for all the needs of the workforce. We want to stress that classroom training is not being eliminated from all training course development. Classroom training now becomes an option, not the only way to deliver training based on the needs and requirements of the learners, course content and learning applications.

From the viewpoint of the participants, self-directed learning is often a method of delivery to help acquire or reinforce skills that they feel will help their personal or professional growth, or both. It would be wise for any organization to review its course offerings to determine which ones can also be offered through self-directed learning methods.

Trainers as Facilitators, Guides, and Mentors

Trainers and training departments have been put in a position to design and deliver courses that meet top priority needs, especially in these two areas:

- the needs of the workforce to receive ongoing training in the ever-changing area of technical proficiency skills

- the needs of the workforce to develop and maintain critical thinking (e.g., planning, reasoning, organizing) skills.

The new mindset for trainers is not what can I teach, but how can I help *facilitate* the learning for the learners? The trainers who will be most successful in the 21st century will be those who quickly adapt to this new mindset. These leading-edge thinkers will uncover ways to deliver education and training when and where the learners need it.

The "new" trainers will be facilitators, mentors, and guides to help the workforce learn on or off the job. They will help each participant by providing subject content and resources and by challenging and guiding before, during, and after the course has been delivered by distance learning. In addition, learners must have a strong support system to aid in both self-directed learning initiatives and the effective use of various distance learning delivery methods.

As training professionals, we know that in order to design and deliver the best courses for our learners, we must first assess their needs. The same holds true for delivering training via distance learning. We will avoid the temptation to jump straight to technology, even though it may seem like the popular thing to do. We'll start this distance learning journey at the beginning and work our way, step-by-step, as every experienced ISD expert would do. We will assess the needs of our workforce and then become "intersector directors." This new phrase means that depending on the training requirements, we will know which direction and technologies to select based on learning content and desired outcomes. After reading this book, we feel that you will have a foundation to provide directions on selecting distance learning technologies.

You and Your Job

We've heard from many trainers that they feel their jobs will be in jeopardy if distance learning is implemented in their organization. Many training functions are, indeed, being outsourced or consolidated in attempts to improve overall human performance while rightsizing organizations. Therefore, trainers need to find ways to develop the mindsets mentioned earlier and find ways to support the training goals of their organization.

Just as human resource managers are now being looked upon as strategic advisers to their companies, training professionals also must be prepared to take on new roles and responsibilities as human performance improvement specialists. In that capacity, they would proactively support the profitable goals and mission of their organizations, and they may be required to assume the roles of analyst, intervention specialist, change manager, and evaluator.

Working as a human performance analyst and intervention specialist, trainers can identify the causes of performance gaps and select appropriate interventions to address the root causes of these gaps. As change managers, trainers can ensure that training interventions such as distance learning are implemented in ways consistent with desired results. As evaluators, trainers can assess the impact these interventions have on overall worker performance.

Trainers have an opportunity to decide that they want not only to learn about distance learning but also to develop creative training solutions to present to their management team. They can uncover new ways of training that are going to meet the demands for information and the acquisition of knowledge. They can select those technologies that will help deliver just-in-time training opportunities for the workforce—wherever it is located. Technological aids and methods of delivery can enhance learning, but they can't replace the human interaction factor needed for successful training and learning experiences.

Training adults requires knowledge of how adults learn and proficiency in selecting the types of support systems that are needed to ensure the success of training efforts and results. Training professionals who have honed their analytical, interpretive, communicative, and facilitative skills are sorely needed to ensure that learner-centered support systems are designed, delivered, and maintained as a critical part of the distance learning process. New roles as training site facilitators are being created, while the traditional training role is being transformed. Every trainer has the opportunity to be creative in exploring ways to become a valuable team member to either design, develop, implement, or maintain distance learning systems of training delivery. It's your choice!

Chapter Two

Distance Learning Master Plan Checklist

Introduction

At the end of this section, we have included two checklists. One is our Master Plan Checklist that we use with the organizations we serve. The other is a checklist of failure factors. We wanted to include them right at the beginning, so that you can benefit from lessons learned as others started on their distance learning journey.

Right Steps, Right Order!

The tendency for some people may be to skip steps they think they have already covered or to start somewhere in the middle. Our advice is to start at the beginning and be sure that you've thoroughly covered each of the following steps before moving on to the next. It's a lesson that many seasoned distance learning professionals had to learn the hard way (us included, as we enthusiastically felt we could jump over a few steps). Our advice: Don't jump ahead! Take it a step at a time. You and your organization will have more reassurance and confidence in moving ahead, knowing that you have covered all the bases in a thorough and professional manner.

Assess the Need for Distance Learning

Do you really need distance learning? Are any of the following statements true: I am operating with a

- decreased training budget
- decreased travel budget
- geographically dispersed workforce.

If you answered true to any of the above statements, you are a prime candidate for distance learning. If you answered false to everything but have a workforce that needs continuous training, distance learning options may be practical considerations in your overall training plan.

Form Your Distance Learning Team

The team approach is a critical component. You should include all key functional stakeholders in your organization—managers, trainers, instructional designers, technical experts, financial decision makers, learners, curriculum planners, and human resource managers. Key stakeholders from both corporate and field activities should be represented on your team. You don't need a cast of many, yet you do want and need a representative from each area. You should assign someone as project director or team leader, or both.

Visit Organizations Currently Using Distance Learning

Distance learning starts on a positive when you and your team have an opportunity to do a site visit to organizations that are already using this type of learning. Some of these organizations are listed in Appendix B. You often don't have to leave your hometown for the visit because many colleges and universities are using distance learning and are proud to show off their systems. Your team visit can include "real" site visits, audio teleconferences, video teleconferences, and attendance at distance learning conferences.

Before you visit, have each team member prepare questions from his or her functional perspective. Each person on the team must feel that his or her needs are being addressed. Members of the host organization may be able to plan a more productive visit for you and your team if you let them know what your questions are before your visit. Sometimes that may not be possible, but if it is, it's a big plus in your favor. Often at the beginning of a distance learning journey, people are not sure what questions to ask. So prepare the ones that you do know and then ask your host, "What were some of the questions and concerns of your trainers? Learners? Instructional designers? Curriculum planners? Technical experts? Finance staff?" Because your hosts had to start at the beginning, just like you, they have many answers to questions that might be important to different members of your team.

Experience It

We feel so strongly about this we've included it as a special section in the book. By experiencing different distance learning events, you will have an opportunity to look at them with two pairs of eyes—first, from the learners' perspective and second, from your perspective as a member of a distance learning team. Perhaps you can participate as individuals with on-line learning from the Internet; attend a satellite event, take part in an audio or video learning teleconference, try a CD-ROM training tool, or the like. Seeing and experiencing distance learning is a step you don't want to miss.

Attend Trade Shows and Vendor Demonstrations

These initiatives will give you an opportunity to play with the equipment without purchasing it! We've included a list of shows and vendors so that you and your team can select which ones you would like to see (Appendix C). As training professionals, we know the value of attending an American Society for Training and Development (ASTD) conference. One of the biggest opportunities is to network with others in our profession and see state-of-the-art presentations and exhibits. You want to give yourself the same opportunity for distance learning. Go where the pros go to learn and keep up-to-date, talk with them about their experiences, perhaps set up site visits or look at training materials that have been designed for different distance learning methods of delivery, and visit the exhibitors. Ask them to tell you the benefits of their products, not only the features (you can get that from product literature). Get lists of clients using their products. If you like what you see, ask the vendors if they would do a demonstration at your organization. Many of the distance learning conferences provide a bound version of the presentation papers for each attendee. These papers can become an important resource for you and your team. And you can use them to be part of a distance learning library or resource center for your organization.

Select Courses

Many trainers ask us which courses are best for distance learning. There is not one answer. To start our distance learning course selection, we use the following as a guidelines. We look at courses that

- are relatively short in length (an hour to a week)
- must be taught to a large population of geographically dispersed workers
- are popular—those that have been well received in on-site delivery or mandated courses like sexual harassment training.

You must have success with your initial offerings because people within the organization will judge distance learning from your initial offerings and delivery. Even though many courses can be converted to distance learning delivery, you don't want to start off with a new course or an unpopular one. Once you have done several popular courses, you can branch out with new offerings.

Assess Learners' Needs

Once you have selected the courses that you want to deliver via distance learning, it is time to assess learners' needs and requirements. Do the learners need to see the trainer [answer this question from the learners' perspectives]? We often hear trainers say, "I must see them." Frequently, this is an emotional need on the part of the trainer, and certainly understandable. Yet, let's go back to the learner-centered mindset. If they need to see you, list the reasons why from their perspective. Do the learners need to answer questions as you deliver your course? Do they need to interact with other learners during the training? Do you need to show visuals such as graphics or videos? Do you have to use a PC? Answering all of these questions for each course will help put you in the best position to select distance learning technologies.

Select Distance Learning Technologies

The cardinal rule is that applications precede the selection of technology. The biggest mistake made in distance learning is selecting a technology before going through all the steps listed above, especially before assessing learners' needs. In the next section, we will list the advantages and disadvantages of using different technologies based on learners' needs and requirements.

Prepare and Present a Cost-Benefit Analysis

Here's where it becomes invaluable to call on the expertise of your team member from finance. Remember to include him or her in from the very beginning. Because every organization, both public and private, must operate in a profitable manner (even though nonprofits don't refer to profit), a carefully prepared cost-justification process will give you the best opportunity to get funding for each phase of your distance learning journey. We decided to include this as a special chapter because this process is such a vital link to turning your wish list into budgeted dollars.

Get Leadership Commitment

You and members of your team will prepare and present briefings to the senior management staff of your organization. You can do this at every stage of planning as you determine what you will do and how you will do it. You will let them know, from the very beginning, why you are taking the steps to learn about and implement distance learning into your strategic training plan. The senior leadership staff must have knowledge of the steps in your distance learning journey. Leadership commitment is vital for your initial and continuous distance learning training plan.

Develop a Strategic Plan

You should have a strategic plan for training in your organization. You will develop a strategic plan for distance learning which will be integrated into your overall plan. What to put into it? See Section Five for the key components to include and how the plan will work for your organization. With this strategic plan and the first 10 steps completed, you will be ready for the next step.

Obtain Funding

You will get the dollars based on a sound journey thus far. Your cost justification will be included in your strategic plan, and at this stage of the process, you will present your plan to get the funding you need for each phase of your program. Don't forget that you have your finance team member who has guided you all along the way and knows what elements will be looked at and why. You will be able to present a rock-solid story of why and how your organization will benefit from utilizing distance learning. Your presentation must tie everything to the bottom line. A well-rehearsed presentation with key members of your distance learning team will help you get funding.

Develop Marketing and Communication Plans

You've got everything lined up, and now it's time to let your world know about distance learning courses that will be offered. Your communication vehicles can include anything and everything possible to effectively and cohesively announce your offerings. You can use e-mail, Internet, a local area network (LAN), a wide area network (WAN), direct mail, in-house brochures, telephone, or fax. Whatever methods you choose, make sure that the content is consistent and benefit oriented and that it highlights the course schedule, course location, registration eligibility, how to register, and of course, the training objectives that will be achieved through taking the course.

It is good to have your graphics department design a logo for your distance learning courses or network operation. You can use this logo on all communication and marketing materials as well as on participant course materials. People will begin to identify with distance learning courses as soon as they see the logo.

Train Personnel

This is a very important part of your success. Many trainers have said to us as we've begun to teach them how to deliver via different methods, "I've done this hundreds of times. I don't need to practice." If you feel this way, please be sure to read Chapter Nineteen in Section Five. The trainer is the key component in successful distance learning delivery. Delivering via different distance learning methods requires knowledge of each method, of preparation and delivery of course material, of interaction with the learners, and of how to help ensure the success of your event. The three key factors that will determine your success are knowledge of the media used, knowledge of how to make it a meaningful learning experience for the learners, and practice.

Develop Pilot Course Design/Conversion

Most courses that are delivered on-site need conversion to distance learning formats. In Section Five the key design and conversion points that are addressed include content length, course length, frequency of delivering all or part of the course by one or more methods, use of multimedia tools, participation exercises and questions, and pre- and post-course work. Evaluations of both content and course delivery methods must be designed to effectively convert and deliver distance learning courses. We have included samples of evaluations other organizations use. Some courses need little conversion, but others may require a complete reworking based on the technology selected for delivery. This point is detailed in Section Five and will help you with general guidelines for the amount of money you will need for course conversion. Course design and conversion costs must be included in your strategic plan.

Conduct Pilot Events

You're on! A synchronized plan that includes coordination with all key people who will play a part in the delivery of your program will help ensure your success. Become familiar with the equipment you will use and practice, practice, practice. Advice from the most successful distance learning trainers includes practice delivering your entire course at least two times prior to actual delivery. If you can have a dry run with a participant at a remote location, that would be terrific! Becoming comfortable with the technology prior to delivery is the biggest favor you can do for yourself. Just do it.

Distance Learning Failure Factors: Lessons Learned

1. Selected technologies before doing a training needs assessment.
2. Did not perform accurate needs assessment.
3. Senior management not involved until too late.
4. No distance learning team put into place.
5. Learners not included on team.
6. Field office representatives not included on team.
7. Finance representatives not included on team.
8. Learner-centered mindset not established and continuously reinforced.
9. System not promoted well internally.
10. Performed poor cost-benefit analysis.
11. Technology did not match perceived application.
12. System not easily accessible to potential users.
13. Overemphasized travel savings.
14. Forgot to include estimated commercial programming costs in budget requests.
15. No top-down endorsement.
16. Concept was not well understood.
17. Little or no emphasis on training users.
18. Role of remote site coordinators not clearly defined.
19. Not enough training and practice by trainers prior to course delivery.
20. System resisted for political reasons.
21. Technology selected not easy to use.
22. No department willing to champion the cause.
23. Poor administrative procedures for registration and scheduling of courses.
24. Too much comparison to on-site training.
25. Selected wrong courses to start distance learning.
26. No fun or humor integrated into learning.
27. No training provided for remote site coordinators.
28. Not enough meaningful interaction between remote site learners and trainers.
29. Remote site learners not given instructions on how to use equipment and interact with the trainer.
30. No follow-up learner support in place.

This checklist contains excerpts from *Defense Technical Information Center: Potential Benefits of Using Video Teleconferencing at AFLC/HQ to Conduct Training*/1988.

Evaluate Pilots

Review the comments from the learners about the content and environment of learning. What worked? What didn't? What can you do to improve the learning environment and outcome for the learners, if anything? Being a good trainer by our own evaluation is not the measurement that is used for distance learning now nor will it be in the 21st century.

The success of distance learning is measured at the remote sites. If the learners are successful in achieving learning outcomes, if they liked this method of learning and can apply the lessons learned, you will have achieved distance learning success.

Distance Learning Master Plan Checklist

- ❑ Assess the need for distance learning.
- ❑ Form your distance learning team.

- ❑ Visit organizations currently using distance learning.
- ❑ Experience it!
- ❑ Attend trade shows and vendor demonstrations.

- ❑ Select courses.
- ❑ Assess learners' needs.
- ❑ Select technologies based on requirements and needs assessment.
- ❑ Prepare cost-benefit analysis.

- ❑ Get leadership commitment.
- ❑ Develop strategic plan.
- ❑ Obtain funding.
- ❑ Develop marketing and communication plans.

- ❑ Train personnel.
- ❑ Develop pilot course design/conversion.
- ❑ Conduct pilot events.
- ❑ Evaluate pilots.

- ❑ Continue course design, conversion, and evaluation.

Continue Course Design, Conversion, and Evaluation

Because you are familiar with the key components of successful on-site training, you can transfer that knowledge to the application of the distance learning component of your training plan. What kind of continuous improvement program is in place for the success of distance learning that is measured at the remote sites? You may want to form a distance learning review team to provide input on and recommendations for new course offerings, suggestions for improving the remote site learning environment for the learners, advice about the effectiveness of the learning for on-the-job applications, and ideas about how different technologies can be used for different parts of course delivery. There is no rule that says you have to select only one method of delivery for a course. You will see that your role as a 21st-century training professional includes thinking of creative ways to engage and support your learners. Think outside of the box because it's a whole new world of options and opportunities.

We conclude this section by providing an easy-to-see Distance Learning Master Plan Checklist. Each main area can be found in the index for information and guidelines on what to do and how to do it. The checklist titled Distance Learning Failure Factors: Lessons Learned on page 16 will help you avoid mistakes right from the start. We will now put the spotlight on different distance learning technologies and how you can use them to achieve your training goals.

Distance Learning Technologies

This section may be your introduction to distance learning technologies, or you may have years of experience and just be looking for a sound review. Regardless of your background, you can feel confident that at the conclusion of this section, you will have an increased understanding of distance learning technologies and how to use them to enhance training.

Two common mistakes are made in the early stages of planning to use distance learning. The first is trying to choose one single technology for all of your organization's training needs. Often this is the result of a persuasive presentation by a vendor demonstrating a solution that will "do it all." (It reminds us of the old Kitchen Magician commercial: "It slices, it dices, it chops, it makes your coffee....")

Organizations that want just one system to work for all distance learning will be disappointed. Imagine asking a carpenter which tool is his favorite. He would probably be very puzzled by your question and ask, "My favorite for what task?" You would be suspect of a carpenter who came to repair your house with only one tool in his toolbox. Abraham Maslow said it best: "He who is good with the hammer thinks that everything is a nail." An effective distance learning program involves the use of a variety of media and technologies based on the requirements and needs of both the learners and the instructor.

The second most common mistake is selecting technologies before identifying training needs and requirements. Selecting technologies before identifying your training needs and requirements is like putting the cart before the horse. **DON'T DO IT! WAIT!** One of us worked with an organization that spent in excess of $4 million on its distance learning program before sitting down and outlining the functional training requirements. Hundreds of thousands of dollars were spent on equipment that did not meet the users' functional requirements.

Let's now look at some of the distance learning tools or technologies that could be a part of your training toolbox.

CHAPTER THREE

Audio Teletraining and Audiographics

INTRODUCTION

Audio teletraining is one of the simplest forms of interactive distance learning. With audio teletraining the learners can hear the instructor and the instructor can hear the learners in an interactive environment. This is done through the use of a device called a convener (see figure 1).

A convener is similar in many ways to a speaker phone. It plugs into a standard telephone wall jack, has a built-in keypad for dialing, and has a speaker that allows all learners to hear the instructor and the learners at other sites. A number of microphones can attach to a single convener, and most of these microphones come equipped with a push-to-talk button. With the push of this button, a learner is able to respond to an instructor's question or seek clarification. The convener and microphones allow many learners to interact directly with an instructor.

Figure 1. Audio Teletraining Convener. An audio teletraining convener is similar in many ways to a speaker phone. Courtesy of A.T. Products, Inc.

Audio teletraining is greatly enhanced with the distribution of prepared learner materials, such as print-based workbooks, videotapes, 35-mm slides, or other audiovisual aids. Instructors can refer learners to these materials as they teach. Resident training courses that already have excellent learner materials are likely candidates for some of your first audio teletraining pilots.

At the beginning of a class, the learners and instructor use the convener to dial into an audio bridge. An audio bridge is a piece of equipment that creates a conference call among the instructor and the learners at all the sites. The audio bridge creates the virtual classroom of sound. Organizations can purchase their own audio bridge or can use bridging services from a number of companies. (See Appendix A for a list of bridging service providers.)

The advantages of audio teletraining are that it is very inexpensive and easy to set up, and the equipment requires minimal instructor or learner training. The obvious disadvantage is that audio teletraining is not appropriate for training that requires the use of live motion video or where visual role modeling is important.

Audio Teletraining Case Study

Dr. Chris Olgren a widely recognized leader in distance education and program manager for the professional certificate program at the University of Wisconsin-Madison, had a learning challenge in addressing the needs of the learners. Because the learners were geographically dispersed, Olgren could select any number of distance learning tools to help achieve the learning goals of the program. Here were the criteria she considered for the

selection process:

1. It needed to be accessible to all the learners.
2. It had to be interactive, active, and collaborative during the learning session.
3. It had to be cost-effective (not expensive for the learners).
4. It had to be a medium in which people could easily participate.
5. It had to fit with the learning objectives.

Olgren selected audio teleconferencing where the equipment each learner needed was a telephone. According to Olgren, "This method of delivery is low tech and very effective. It is not 'gee whiz' technology, however, we have effectively taught over 30,000 learners with audio teleconferencing." Here s how it works:

At least two weeks prior to the seminar, learners receive a complete package of course materials, which contains

- a welcome letter
- a handbook of readings and print resources
- a pre-seminar reading assignment
- an interactive workbook or worksheets
- seminar instructions for dialing into the central number
- teleconferencing pointers or ground rules
- seminar agenda
- roster of participants
- seminar evaluation form.

Learners dial into the central number, and a roll call is taken to confirm the participation of enrolled learners. The ground rules are explained, and then the seminar begins. The presenter or presenters are all subject matter experts, and they build in participation activities every five or 10 minutes. Each seminar lasts approximately two hours, and each learner is expected to write a report after the session in order to earn continuing education units (CEU) toward certification.

When asked about some aspects of the program she was particularly proud of, Olgren said, "I have pride in this method because from the perspective of the learners, it has been very effective. The feedback from the learners is that it is a useful tool for the Certificate Program. It provides a model for their own work in audio teleconferencing, and learners gain practical information they can apply in their organizations." The learners complete an evaluation form in a print format. There is a scale of effectiveness from 1 (poor) to 5 (excellent) with different questions based on the content, expectations, and learning experience. The average evaluation comes in at 4.2. She goes on to say that if she could change one aspect of the program, it would be to "work more closely with the presenters. They are content experts on their subject but may not be well versed in audio teleconference techniques. They need to know tips on how to design their presentation (this does not come naturally), pros and cons of this medium, how to design for active learning and how to humanize the learning environment." A key here is to ensure that you train the trainers to create course materials, participation exercises, and content delivery all tailored to an audio teleconference environment where you can't see the learners and they can't see you.

Audio Teletraining: Distance Learning Technical Summary

Conference-call interaction with the instructor, and learners able to speak with and hear each other through the use of speakerphone or convener. Usually accompanied by learner materials distributed before the seminar.

Advantages	Disadvantages
Very inexpensive	Not appropriate for training requiring live interactive video
Easy to set up	Requires pre-distribution of visual materials
Minimal training on equipment	
Uses existing phone lines	

What advice would Olgren give to the readers of the book? The two most important things she wants you to do are to design the content for interactive learning and drop preconceived notions of what technologies are best for distance learning. This method is often overlooked because it is not high tech. Don t overlook audio teleconferencing as an excellent method of delivery.

Olgren reminds us that another advantage of audio teleconferencing is that you can begin distance learning on a smaller budget than other types of distance learning. As a creative trainer, this allows you to begin or enhance your course offerings without busting the budget.

Audiographics

Audiographics take audio teletraining one step further. In addition to learners and the instructor being able to interact in a so-called audio classroom, they are able to share computer-generated graphics and slides. Audiographics training requires that the instructor and learner sites have the equipment needed for audio teletraining as well as a personal computer (PC), audiographics software, a special modem, and an interaction tablet (see figure 2).

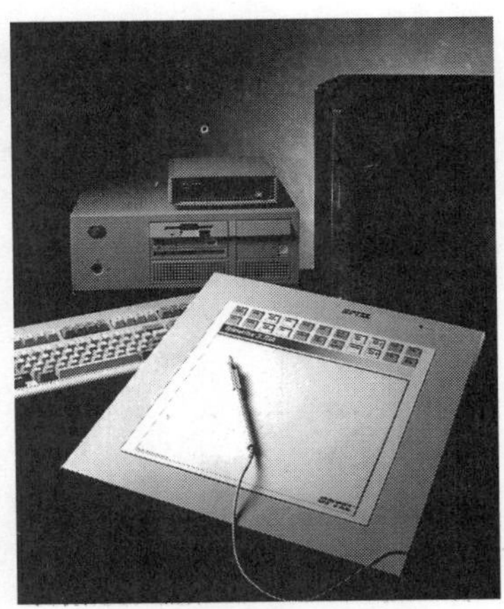

Figure 2. Audiographic System. An audiographic system brings computer graphics to the audio classroom. Courtesy of Optel Communications, Inc.

The personal computer, software, and interaction tablet allow the learners and instructor to create graphics and share them with each site. The interaction tablet performs many of the same functions as a computer mouse, allowing the user to select menu items as well as annotating slides that are being displayed on screen. It is similar to the device that broadcaster John Madden uses while providing commentary on televised football games. He draws Xs and Os on the TV screen to explain the plays visually. In training, this device allows the instructor or learner to emphasize a key area of a slide or chart to increase comprehension.

The modem used in audiographics training is similar to modems that are commonly sold with PCs. It allows the graphics to be transmitted from the PC over phone lines to the audio bridge and from the audio bridge to the other PCs. Unlike other PCs, the graphics modem allows both the computer graphics and the voice of the instructor or learner to be transmitted simultaneously over the same phone line.

A class that uses audiographics is initiated the same way as an audio teletraining class. The learners and instructor use the convener to dial into the audio bridge.

The instructor then uses the interaction tablet to control what the learners at remote sites are seeing on their PC monitors.

The advantages of audiographics are that they are relatively inexpensive and easy to set up and that they require moderate training for an instructor and minimal training for learners. They also enable learners and the instructor to share graphics and charts in a real-time environment. The disadvantage is that like audio teletraining, it is not appropriate for training that requires the use of live motion video or where visual role modeling is important.

Audiographics Case Study

Today's marketplace is one in which corporations and organizations must interact and compete in an international environment. With this expansion of the marketplace comes new training requirements. IBM, GE Medical Systems, and General Motors are among a number of companies that found that a select number of their English-speaking scientists and engineers at varied locations needed skills in reading technical documents written in Japanese. Fortunately, these companies were able to partner with the Department of Engineering Professional Development at the University of Wisconsin-Madison and provide a way for employees to receive the needed training without having to leave their workplace. Through an effective application of audiographics distance learning, Professor Jim Davis and his team offer several courses each year for those needing this special skill.

In evaluating which distance learning media they might use to offer the Technical Japanese Program, Davis's department had established several criteria, including the following:

- ability to view what learners were writing
- ease of inputting materials through use of scanner
- ease of presenting material
- ease of use of equipment required
- low capital cost so learners could participate from home if necessary.

Based on the above criteria, they chose audiographic conferencing as the delivery method. The equipment required at the remote sites was very minimal. In many cases the equipment was already in-house at the corporate site. Where it was not, the corporations either purchased the equipment or were able to rent it locally for $100 to 200 per month. The equipment at each site consisted of

- computer
- audiographics software
- graphics tablet (allows a learner's writing to be displayed)
- modem
- audioconferencing system
- two regular phone lines.

One of the essential components in any distance learning program is an evaluation of the effectiveness of the instruction. In the five years that the Technical

Japanese Program has been offered via distance learning, a number of studies have been done to compare the performance of learners at remote sites with those at the Madison campus. Consistently since its first offering, an analysis of examination scores has shown no statistical difference (at the 5 percent level) between the two groups. Figure 3 illustrates the mean examination scores for several semesters.

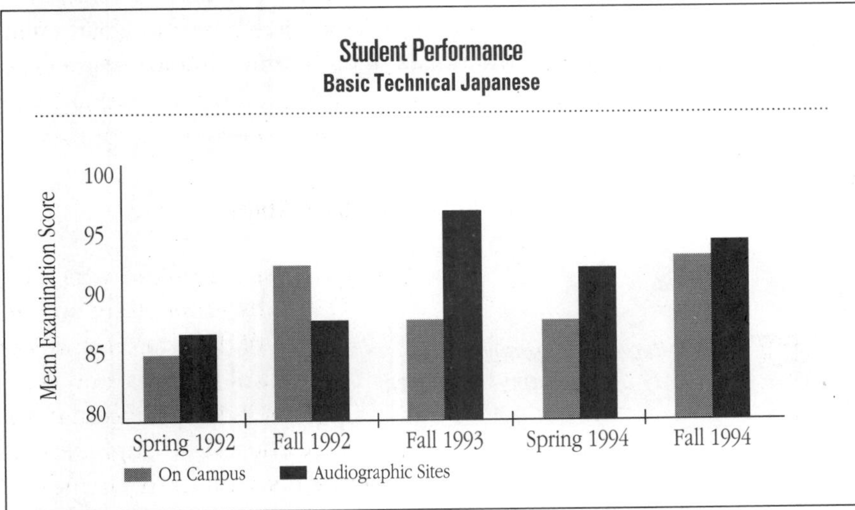

Figure 3. Student Performance in Technical Japanese Course. Mean examination scores show no statistical difference between learners on campus and at audiographic sites.

It is easy to understand why Jim Davis and his team are especially proud of taking what is an admittedly difficult language and teaching it successfully through this medium. It has been extremely rewarding for them to see learners from varied corporations progress from reading absolutely no Japanese to being able to read and understand technical documents. This new skill has enabled these employees to exchange technical information with Japanese partners and to better monitor advances by Japanese competitors.

Davis said he would advise readers to consider audiographic conferencing as a mainstream distance learning technology. "When we started, I originally thought that the audiographic method of delivery would be replaced by video teleconferencing," Davis said. "Later, I found that many of the corporate remote sites would not schedule their VTC room or equipment for training. It was reserved for meetings and they were hesitant to block off four hours at a time, several times per month for this course." Now he finds that training via audiographic conferencing is growing and that the flexibility the system allows makes it a better choice for his courses even when other forms of delivery are available.

Audiographics: Distance Learning Technical Summary

Conference-call audio interaction coupled with ability for the instructor and learners to share computer-generated graphics and slides with each other in a live interactive mode.

Advantages	Disadvantages
Very inexpensive	Not appropriate for training requiring live interactive video
Easy to set up	May require pre-distribution of computer image files
Minimal training on equipment	Requires some degree of computer literacy to create course materials
Uses existing phone lines	
Ability to share charts, graphs, digitized photos	
Whiteboard capability	

The Technical Japanese Program via audiographics is an excellent model for others to follow. It is a case involving a new training requirement emerging as a result of the expanding global marketplace. It is an example of partnering between the corporate and academic sectors to meet that requirement. And it is a pattern for others to emulate in choosing a particular distance learning technology based on the needs of the learners and a desire of the instructors to best meet those needs.

CHAPTER FOUR

Interactive Television

INTRODUCTION

Interactive television is the most widely used distance learning technology when the training audience is dispersed over a large geographic area and when live motion video is required. It is sometimes called business television or video teletraining. The learners can both see and hear the instructor by watching a television monitor. It is different from static television in that the instructor receives immediate feedback from the learners either from an audio system (yes, it is the same system as audio teletraining), keypad viewer response system, telephone, fax, or a combination of the above.

KEYPAD VIEWER RESPONSE SYSTEM AND INSTRUCTOR CONSOLE

The keypad viewer response system is a device about the size of a desktop calculator (see figure 4). Usually a keypad is at each learner's desk. The keypad has alphanumeric keys that allow each learner to input information that is then transmitted to the instructor site. At the beginning of each class, for example, learners usually use the keypad to input their identification number or their name. Some viewer response pads also have a built in microphone, which consolidates the convener and the viewer response pad.

Figure 4. Viewer Response Pad.
The keypad viewer response system lets learners input information. Courtesy of One Touch Systems, Inc.

The instructor has a console that displays the names of the learners and their responses to questions (see figure 5). For example, the instructor might ask a multiple choice question, and the learners would use the keypads to respond. The instructor can then view either the overall response (how many answered A, how many B, and so on) or the individual responses (Mr. Smith's answer). The console also provides a visual cue to the instructor when a learner presses the call button to ask a question. (A little icon with a raised hand appears on his screen!)

So, you have the learners watching television at a number of geographically separated classrooms located throughout your area of training responsibility. They have a push-to-talk microphone and a keypad viewer response system in front of them. As the instructor conducts the training, he or she may ask, "Ms. Smith, what do you think about what we just talked about?" and Ms. Smith uses her microphone to respond. The instructor asks a question and then adjusts the instruction to the level of comprehension the learners demonstrated by the responses they provide with their viewer response keypads.

Figure 5. Instructor Console for Viewer Response System.
Learners' answers are visible on their instructors' console. Courtesy of One Touch Systems, Inc.

The equipment needed at the remote sites for interactive television is fairly simple. Almost all interactive television networks use satellite delivery to transmit instructors' video and audio. This then requires a satellite dish (see figure 6 on the next page) at the learner site (often called the downlink site) to receive the electrons coming from the instructor's site. A satellite receiver then turns those instructor electrons into a signal that the television understands. Of course, a television is needed to turn that signal into something learners can view and hear. Learners need a convener and microphones to provide verbal responses back to the instructor. And if you desire to share data information, you need a viewer response pad system.

The equipment needed at the instructor site (often called the uplink site) can be extremely simple or get rather complex. In the absolute simplest configuration, it requires a piece of paper called a contract with a service provider. You provide the instructor and course content, and the service provider furnishes all of the other "stuff" necessary to uplink your instructor electrons to a satellite where the learner sites can then receive them using the satellite dish and other equipment. (See Appendix A for a list of commercial and government interactive television uplink providers.) We recommend that you use a service provider for your first interactive television distance learning event.

Figure 6. Satellite Downlink Dish.
A satellite downlink dish receives the audio and video signal from the instructor's site. Courtesy AT&T Tridom.

Now let's consider some of the equipment required in a permanent interactive television network. There are two different paradigms as to what is required. The first is a television studio paradigm. From this point of view, you need a full broadcast television studio complete with crew and broadcast-quality equipment.

The second paradigm is one of an instructional classroom studio. It is a point of view that can best be summarized in the phrase "form follows functions." It proposes that content is the most important component and that degree of broadcast quality in distance learning is not the same as that required for broadcast television.

As you would guess, the proponents of the television studio paradigm usually had years of experience in broadcast television. Because they have spent a great deal of time focused on getting that perfectly clean powerful signal, they do not want anything less for the learners. It is good to have folks who are concerned with the quality of the electron signal that learner sites are receiving.

The proponents of the classroom studio often come from an instructional design background. From their view, if the instructional component is designed well, learners will not notice that the instructor is flipping his own slides and that a studio engineer isn't causing the graphics to display on cue. It is good to have folks who are concerned with the quality of the instructional design of a distance learning event.

What you will find is that many of the equipment components for both paradigms are the same. The difference is in the degree of quality. For example, in both paradigms you need a camera to visually capture what the instructor is doing. A broadcast studio television camera can cost $75,000 to $150,000. An instructional quality classroom camera costs $7,500 to $15,000. What is the difference? The quality of the signal captured. So it is with many of the components necessary for interactive television. The functionality is the same, and the difference is in the degree of quality desired or needed. With that in mind, let's look at specific components that are necessary at the instructor site, regardless of the degree of quality needed.

We have already mentioned a video camera. In its simplest form, it resembles a camcorder minus the video recording capability. The camera lens becomes the eyes of the learners. It is through this lens that the learners are able to observe the instructor. There are a multitude of choices when selecting the camera. Do you want one that is remote controlled by the instructor, or will a camera person be operating it? Is a broadcast-quality signal required, or will the quality of picture that you get from a high-end camcorder suffice? What amount of zoom do you require? **Don't worry about these questions at this time!** You do not need to know how to differentiate between two video signals displayed on an electronic oscilloscope (a gee whiz device that measures video signal quality to the nth degree). What you do need to understand is this: At the instructor site you have a camera. It captures a video image of the instructor and sends it to a device called a video mixer.

The video mixer is a piece of equipment that allows several different video sources to be connected to it. The instructor or studio technician can then select which signal is sent to the learners. In addition to the camera mentioned above, what are some other possible video sources? How about a VCR? You probably have existing videotapes that are valuable teaching aids in conducting a class. The VCR would be another video signal that would be connected to the video mixer. The video signal from a personal computer is another common source that is connected to the video mixer. The instructor can then use computer-generated graphics or the actual live display of a computer program. This is very beneficial in software application training.

If the camera lens is the eyes of the learners, then the microphone becomes the learners' ears. The most common microphone for interactive television is a lapel mike that clips onto the instructor's clothing. The microphone picks up the instructor's voice and sends it to an audio mixer.

The audio mixer is the sound equivalent of the video mixer. The audio mixer has a number of audio sources connected to it. In addition to the instructor's microphone, other possible audio sources include an audiocassette player, a compact disc player, or additional microphones. The instructor or studio technician can select which audio signal, or combination of audio signals, is sent to the learner sites.

The signals from the video mixer and the audio mixer are routed to the satellite uplink dish. Remember a satellite dish receives the interactive television signal at the learner, or downlink, site. At the instructor (uplink) site, an uplink dish sends the signal up to a satellite so that it can be received by the learner sites. There are analog uplink dishes, and there are digital uplink dishes (see Glossary). There are C-Band and there are Ku-band dishes. There are round dishes and elliptical dishes. Don't worry about these differences right now. The key point is that at the instructor site the electrons that represent what the teacher is doing or saying go through the video mixer and audio mixer and then end up being beamed to the heavens via this satellite uplink dish.

Figure 7. Audiovisual Console.
Console for controlling audiovisual equipment.
Courtesy PictureTel, Inc.

As you can see, there are a number of components at the instructor site. You might wonder if you need an army of technicians to help operate the different equipment. Fortunately, technology has a simple solution. The instructor can control these components by using a touch-screen control panel that operates in much the same way as an ATM machine. (However, we have never seen a touch-screen panel that dispenses cash!). Instructors who want to play a videotape, for example, touch the panel on the square or picture icon that says "VCR." The touch-screen control panel then displays the familiar VCR control functions—play, stop, rewind, fast forward, and the like—and the instructor can operate the VCR through the panel (see figure 7 on page 29). An important difference between this and the familiar VCR panel is that after a power interruption this one doesn't blink "12:00, 12:00, 12:00..." This control panel does provide a user-friendly way to control equipment such as the camera, video mixer, audio mixer, VCR, and other components found at the instructor site.

The advantages of interactive television include the ability to transmit the training to a large number of sites at one time, high-quality video and audio signals, cost-efficiencies when dealing with a large number of sites, and the ability to use many of the distance learning facilities that are capable of receiving interactive television events. The disadvantages are the cost of the equipment necessary to uplink the signal, the complexity of the uplink equipment, and the training required at remote sites to ensure quality reception of the signal and quality return audio.

Interactive Television Case Study

UNISYS

Imagine this: Your training department has just received a mandate to train over 7,500 people in the United States on the Microsoft Office Suite products. The mandate includes doing it quickly and in a cost-effective manner. Quick, what do you do? And how do you go from no experience in distance learning to winning an award for Best Distance Learning Program—Corporate Training from the United States Distance Learning Association? Ask Unisys, a global leader in providing information management solutions. The company made it happen by providing desktop application satellite-delivered instruction without PCs at the remote site classrooms.

The training challenges. The key challenges were to

- deliver cost-effective training to over 7,500 employees
- train U.S.-based employees on Microsoft Word for Windows 6.0, PowerPoint 4.0, Excel 5.0, and other topics including Microsoft Mail and Lotus Notes
- train everyone in a thorough and consistent fashion
- enable the learners to interact with the instructors
- train everyone in a short period of time.

To see how these challenges were met, Karen Mantyla went to the Unisys corporate headquarters in Blue Bell, Pennsylvania. This visit was prompted by Mantyla seeing Kathleen Muldoon's presentation about the Unisys case study at the ASTD annual conference in 1996. The training appeared to be a trainer's nightmare turned dream-come-true. Here's how the company did it.

The critical component: a team approach. The overriding message from Kathy Muldoon and the executives at Unisys is that it takes a team, right from the start. The power of the Unisys team turned the thoughts from "it won't work," to "it will work," to "it does work," according to Muldoon. This case study is a benchmark for others to use as they look to satellite-based instruction to meet the cost-effective training needs and requirements of a large, geographically dispersed workforce.

The delivery system. The Unisys Business Television (UBT) Network was already in place prior to receiving the mandate to train more than 7,500 people in the Microsoft products. Through the initial initiatives and funding by the marketing department, the satellite network could broadcast to 95 U.S. and 43 European Unisys facilities.

Also, and extremely important, the network could provide remote site learners with interactivity options. At 51 U.S. locations, the One Touch student response pads were already in place. This meant that learners at all of those locations could talk to the instructor, ask questions, and be tested on application knowledge. At the other sites, there was a telephone for live call-in questions and a fax machine to send both questions and comments to the instructor located at the headquarters origination site. The network, at this point, had been used to meet specific ongoing communication needs for the internal workforce and more than 50,000 clients in over 100 countries. A great use, but now it was time to look at this system to help meet mandated training challenges.

The interactive distance learning team members. Fortunately for the trainers, the Unisys Business Network is led by creative and entrepreneurial thinkers. Steve Fanelli, director of Unisys Television Services, fully supported the use of UBT for the "highway" to deliver the training. Garrett Lohne, UBT senior producer and director, was part of the new distance learning team. Note that commitment by senior leadership is extremely important in any distance learning initiative and according to Lohne, Steve Fanelli provided that total commitment to support the success of this new pioneering training venture. The core team members included

- team leader, Kathy Muldoon (senior education consultant, information technology)
- project manager, Frank Weiss
- curriculum planner, Jim Bacho
- UBT producer and director, Garrett Lohne

These team members utilized the talents of both internal and external training consultants (curriculum planners and instructors) to ensure that the teamwork represented the key needs and requirements from both ends of the camera—the learners and the instructors.

Remote site equipment. The remote sites had no PCs. Yes, computer training was about to be designed without any hands-on application during the instruction. Each classroom had a TV monitor with learner response systems—either One Touch Learner Response Pads or a telephone and a fax machine for live interaction.

The instruction. The on-site training program for each subject consisted of six one-hour sessions on consecutive Tuesdays. The curriculum planners took the lead to convert each course for interactive distance learning via satellite. They designed each course in the desktop application series to include learner participation in the live broadcast (building in interaction activities and exercises every five to seven minutes with games, comments, quizzes, and questions) and development of a participant guide, which included an exercise disk, computer-based training, references, tips, and self-directed information in a beginner-to-advanced format. Each course broadcast was one hour per week for six weeks. Because the remote site learners did not have PCs during the live instruction, trainers gave them practice exercises as homework between each broadcast session of the course. At the beginning of each broadcast, the learners were quizzed on the homework from the week before.

The instructors. The instructors chosen for this method of delivery would go from an average, single site classroom size of 25 learners to a virtual nationwide classroom with 1,000 learners. The instructors were chosen by videotaped audition held in the interactive distance learning (IDL) studio. The qualities needed were sense of humor, flexibility, spontaneity, adaptability, and enthusiasm in front of the camera. Of course, being a good instructor on-site was the prerequisite for being a good instructor for interactive distance learning. Garrett trained the instructors on TV presentation skills, teaching to the camera (the eyes of the learners), and integrating interactivity with the equipment in the IDL studio. The IDL studio was a room with two desk modules—one desk for the instructor and one for the host of each broadcast. The host operated the One Touch System Controller (see picture on page 27) to set up, administer, and control all interactivity: questions, comments, and quizzes.

Cost per learner for training. The estimated cost was based on the projected number of learners for each course in the series. The Unisys team expected that there would be approximately 800 learners per broadcast, and its projected cost was $125 per learner, per broadcast. With almost 1,200 learners registered for each broadcast, the actual cost per learner was $41.

Evaluation tools and assessment results. A sample of the evaluation form used to assess the success of both the learning outcomes and method of delivery is shown on pages 33–34. The great news is that the productivity of the learners for the desktop applications increased by 20 percent as a result of the course. Comments from the remote site participants also reflected an overwhelming enjoyment of receiving training via interactive distance learning. They liked it, they learned their lessons well, and it was totally cost-effective for Unisys, a truly winning combination.

After Unisys won the award from the United States Distance Learning Association, Garrett Lohne commented, "It isn't enough for trainers in the '90s to limit their delivery methods to classroom or computer-based training/self-study. Satellite-delivered training, like the Unisys IDL effort, works easily into employees' schedules, provides the live instruction, and offers high levels of live interactivity between instructor and learner. Besides, when you look at what it typically costs to send someone to training anywhere, it's hard to beat."

UNISYS

DESKTOP IDL EVALUATION
For Word for Windows 6.0–Program 6

SAMPLE LAYOUT

SITE LOCATION ____________________

ORG. NAME ____________________ **NAME (OPTIONAL)** ____________________

Your input is extremely valuable in assisting us to evaluate the effectiveness of this program. Please read each statement carefully and circle the appropriate response. When complete, double fold this sheet on the dotted line with the return address exposed. Staple and return using Unisys interoffice mail.

General Information

A. Please match your job to the closest category provided.

Manager/Supervisor	Technical/Professional	Administrative Professional
Direct Sales	Non-Exempt Technical	Non-Exempt Admin./Clerical
Non-Exempt Other		

B. What (if anything) keeps you from using your PC to effectively perform you job responsibilities? (Choose all that apply)

Lack of time	Lack of training	No management support for training
Inadequate hardware	Inadequate software	Other: ____________________

C. Assess your current knowledge of Word for Windows 6.0.

Novice	Intermediate	Expert

Broadcast Session Evaluation

	Strongly Agree				Strongly Disagree
1. This session was time well spent in discovering practical and useful ideas and techniques.	5	4	3	2	1
2. The length of the session (1 hour) is appropriate.	5	4	3	2	1
3. The facilitator(s) presented the material in a clear and understanding manner.	5	4	3	2	1
4. Questions I had during the broadcast were answered.	5	4	3	2	1

5. Did you find this session informative?	Yes	No	Undecided
6. Did you learn something useful during this session?	Yes	No	Undecided
7. Will you attend the next program session?	Yes	No	Undecided
8. Would you recommend this course to others?	Yes	No	Undecided

continued on next page

UNISYS **INTEROFFICE MAIL**

Please return this evaluation to:

Attention: Mary McAdoo

Location: Blue Bell

To return: Double fold using this dotted line, with above address exposed, and staple.

Post-Broadcast Session Evaluation:
Please complete the follow questions after using the exercises, CBT, and/or references.

	Strongly Agree				Strongly Disagree
9. I was motivated by the program to complete the exercises at my desk.	5	4	3	2	1
10. The materials were well designed to complement the session presentation.	5	4	3	2	1
11. The exercises helped to reinforce my learning on each topic.	5	4	3	2	1
12. The CBT, include with the package, helped to reinforce my learning on each topic.	5	4	3	2	1
13. The references to the QUE book, CBT, and On-Line HELP were a valuable part of the program.	5	4	3	2	1

14. What percent of your total working time will be spent on tasks that require the skill/knowledge presented in the course? (Circle one)

 0 10 20 30 40 50 60 70 80 90 100

15. Rate your productivity, **before** this learning experience, on your job tasks that required the skill/knowledge presented in the course (100 percent represents highest productivity; 50 percent means that you could complete the tasks half as well, or half as fast).

 0 10 20 30 40 50 60 70 80 90 100

16. Rate your productivity, (future project) **after** this learning experience, on your job tasks that require the skills/knowledge presented in the course (100 percent represents highest productivity; 50 percent means that you could complete the tasks half as well, or half as fast).

 0 10 20 30 40 50 60 70 80 90 100

Interactive Television: Distance Learning Technical Summary

Learners see and hear the instructor by viewing live television. Instructor receives feedback and interacts with learners through an audio connection or a viewer response keypad, or a combination of both.

Advantages	Disadvantages
Ability to transmit live video and audio to multiple sites in widely dispersed locations	Requires extensive equipment to broadcast signal
Significant cost-efficiencies for large audiences	Requires installation of satellite downlink dishes at remote sites
Large inventory of facilities already in place available for use	Requires thorough training on equipment at remote sites
When used with viewer response pads, allows data input from learners	

Chapter Five

Video Teleconferencing

Introduction

Video teleconferencing has been used for several years in lieu of face-to-face meetings, primarily among a small number of sites. However, it now has become one of the more common methods of training at a distance as well. The learners can see and hear the instructor, and the instructor can see and hear the learners. It is sometimes referred to as "two way, two way," referring to the two-way transmission of both an audio and a video signal.

Figure 8. Video Teleconferencing System.
With a video teleconferencing system, equipment may be the same at the instructors' and learners' sites. Courtesy PictureTel, Inc.

With video teleconferencing, the equipment is often the same at both the instructor or source site and the learner or remote sites. This provides the flexibility for any of the sites within the system to become an instructor site. Let's look at some of the equipment typically found within a video teleconferencing classroom (see figure 8).

Cameras at each site capture what the instructor or learners are doing. There are usually three cameras: one oriented toward where an instructor would sit, a second overhead camera directed where the instructor would put visual aids (paper slides or three-dimensional objects), and a third camera pointed where the learners sit. The cameras can be controlled by those physically at the site or by someone at one of the remote sites. An instructor may choose to limit the remote site control of cameras to only certain preset views.

A remote control, similar to that for a TV or VCR, allows an instructor or learner to choose which camera is displayed as well as the camera's angle or zoom control. A number of other devices are also available to control cameras automatically. One device causes the camera to automatically zoom in on whoever is talking. Another device, the wand device, can be easily handed from one individual to another and causes the camera to zoom in on the person holding it.

A camera's video signal is fed to the "brains" of the site, an electronic box called a codec, short for coder/decoder. The codec takes that signal along with the audio signal from classroom microphones and changes them to digital information. All that means is that instead of a signal that our TV sets would understand, the video and audio signals are changed to 1s and 0s that represent the sights and sounds of the classroom. This information is then sent, usually over high-capacity phone lines, to the remote sites. After they have received the digital information, the codec at those sites converts the digital signal back to a signal that can be displayed on a television monitor.

Two large television monitors allow people at the sites to see both what the cameras at their own site (outgoing video) are seeing and what the cameras at the remote site (incoming video) are seeing.

Other audiovisual sources can also be linked into the codec. Most sites are equipped with a VCR so that a videotape can be viewed and the signal transmitted to the other sites. A special type of 35-mm slide projector commonly used at video teleconference sites displays slides as video signals that are fed into the codec and not as images that go through a lens to a wall or screen. This technology allows the use of existing archives of 35-mm slides during an instruction or training period.

In the chapter on interactive television, we referred to a touch-screen control panel that the instructor could use to control the various audiovisual components at the source site. This same type of control is often used with video teleconferencing as well. It enables the instructor to switch easily among different audiovisual devices and cameras without having to juggle an armful of remote controls.

The advantages of video teleconferencing are that learners and instructors can see each other and that any site in the system may be an instructor origination site. The disadvantages include the high costs for establishing the required transmission lines and equipment.

Video Teleconferencing Case Study

How do you provide training to new recruiters at hundreds of field offices throughout the continental United States, Hawaii, and Puerto Rico? Management Recruiters International (MRI), Inc., had existing training packages that local franchisees used to train newly hired recruiters. The training packages consisted primarily of printed course materials and videotapes. The franchisees used these materials to conduct training sessions locally. However, the pace of hiring new employees and the time required to train them soon taxed the ability of the local franchisees to perform other functions.

Jerry Hill, vice president of training, and Chuck Vazac, director of videoconferencing, turned to distance learning via video teleconferencing as a way to help the local franchisees and at the same time to maximize new recruiters' opportunities for success. "We were attending Telecon [one of the primary industry trade shows for distance learning] when the idea came to us," said Vazac? "We had an existing video teleconferencing network. It was used as a competitive advantage to allow employers to interview potential recruits without the need for travel." He continued: "We saw presentations from some of the training networks, and it hit us. Why not use our existing videoconferencing network for training as well as interviewing?"

MRI's network, ConferView, will exceed 300 sites in 1997. The initial training application, account executive basic training, was tremendously successful. It provided the new recruiters with the skills they needed to get a fast start on productivity. Chuck Vazac explained: "We would have a class in the morning on a particular topic, for example, telephone sales prospecting. The employees would then take a break from the training to immediately apply the skill. The class would come back online after a few hours and discuss how it went and what could be done to improve." In addition to freeing the franchisees from the requirement to provide this initial training (they say it is the "best thing ever done!"), the distance learning course had an additional benefit—the retention rate for new recruiters tripled!

The new recruiters also feel part of a larger organization when they participate in training this way. Rather than thinking that their organization is restricted to the local office personnel and staff, they get to interact with personnel at other offices and the staff at corporate headquarters in Cleveland, Ohio. This corporate bonding also resulted in increased interoffice productivity. MRI discovered that the new recruiters more easily shared sales referrals with other offices where their video classmates worked.

What areas of the distance learning initiative are the trainers particularly proud of? Vazac said, "We take pride in winning the U.S. Distance Learning Association Award for Best Distance Learning Network Under Two Years Old. We were pleased to be recognized in a field that is largely dominated by academic institutions. To be a corporate organization and win the award was especially gratifying. It is also rewarding to read the learner evaluation forms and to know that they feel better trained and better prepared for their job as a result of this effort." This type of learner-centered approach helps to explain the success of ConferView.

The training offerings have continued to grow. Hill realized that corporate headquarters was in no way the sole repository of good trainers. He tapped the skills of franchisees by instituting a training program called the Best Practices Forum. Using ConferView, franchisees from various offices began to offer sessions that all offices could benefit from, including courses on developing local market share, prioritizing job orders, training administrative assistants, and business writing.

Readers who are considering video teleconferencing should focus on the power of the application and not on the minor differences between various video teleconferencing equipment, according to Vazac. "I've seen some folks agonize for months between two very similar video teleconferencing systems that had minor differences," he said. Vazac believes that choosing one of the mainstream systems that meets industry standards and getting on with the power of using it is preferable to trying to find the "perfect system."

Training via video teleconferencing has been a catalyst in enabling MRI to provide needed skills to its employees nationwide. Vazac attributes the increase in recruiter retention and productivity directly to MRI's distance learning initiative. He said, "The recruiters are more likely to succeed if they get the needed training quickly. ConferView has enabled us to get them that training and help them succeed. It is a lot harder to retain a struggling recruiter than one who is well trained and quickly experiencing positive results. We now have many more of the latter."

Video Teleconferencing: Distance Learning Technical Summary

Two-way transmission of both video and audio that allows the learners to see and hear the instructor and the instructor to both see and hear the learners.

Advantages	Disadvantages
Allows the instructor to see the learners	High costs for transmission of courses
Flexibility of multiple "instructor" sites	High costs for establishing sites
Enables learners to interact with each other visually	Difficulty of managing visual interaction with several sites

CHAPTER SIX

Computer-Based Training

INTRODUCTION

One of the fastest growing areas in distance learning is interactive computer-based training. Within the past few years, there have been tremendous advances in multimedia personal computers. Even the least expensive personal computers now have the ability to play full-motion video clips, provide stereo sound, and access tremendous amounts of information that are stored on CD-ROM disks.

Additionally, multimedia authoring software has become more economical and easier to use. Previously, creating multimedia computer-based training presentations required a staff of programmers who wrote cryptic codes for several weeks. The new authoring software allows users to point and click rather than write programming codes.

As a result of these two advances, many organizations are producing computer-based training (CBT) programs of courses that had been taught in a classroom environment, and they are teaching the same material and achieving the same objectives. If you have not been to one of the computer superstores in the last year, go sometime this week. Ask for a demonstration of some of the multimedia software commercially available. As you watch the demonstration, ask yourself, "What material or courses do we train that might be taught using this type of media?"

CBT has a broad range of complexity. At one end of the spectrum, it may be fairly simple, mostly text with a few still graphics. At the other end, it may include live video clips, sound, and animations. Figure 9 is a screen from a fairly complex CBT program. Regardless of whether it is fairly simple text or a mix of multimedia, quality CBT includes assessment features and branching capabilities that allow for self-paced instruction based on an individual's level of proficiency and ability to grasp the subject matter being presented. These features prevent trainees from having to page through screens full of information with which they are already familiar. This functionality of assessment and branching can be a real asset when you have a training audience that varies greatly in its knowledge of an area.

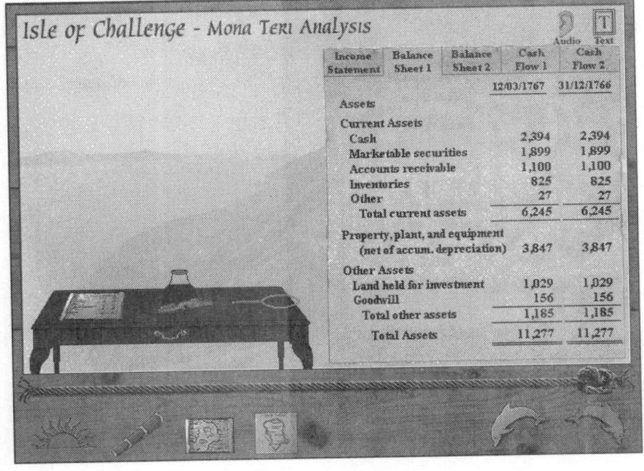

Figure 9. Screen-capture from "Interpreting Basic Financial Statements" CBT Program.
Courtesy EDS Corporation.

What is needed to use CBT? The one piece of equipment the learner needs is a multimedia PC (MPC), which allows use of interactive software that may include video clips, sound, and animations. The PC industry lists the capabilities a multimedia PC should have in its MPC standard. As technology advances, more capabilities are built in a multimedia PC, and the MPC standard changes. Initially, the standard was simply MPC, then along came the improved MPC standard, which was MPC2. Next was MPC3...and you get the idea. Check with your technical support personnel for the current MPC standard and the capabilities associated with it.

Even though the capabilities improve, price remains fairly constant. For between $2,000 and $2,500, you can purchase the current generation multimedia PC. You may be tempted to wait, thinking that the price of technology will drop. You are absolutely right—it will! Six months to a year from the time you purchase it, there will be new and improved multimedia PCs, which will cause the price of the previous generation to decrease. However, you must factor in the lost opportunities that come from waiting. There will always be something new. Try to focus on your existing training requirements and meet them now. You can reevaluate periodically. In many cases, you may find that the improvement from one generation PC to the next does not necessarily affect your training outcome.

Developing and creating the multimedia software requires additional computer equipment and proficiency with the authoring software. Do you already have staff personnel who develop course materials for classroom instruction, or do you contract those tasks out? If you are already staffed with instructional designers and course developers, you may be able to give them new tools and additional training that would enable them to create computer-based training programs. Appendix A lists some of the more widely used multimedia authoring software. Some of the software companies conduct special training for users of their product. (Makes sense. What good is a great piece of software if folks don't know how to use it?) Other software vendors have a list of authorized training representatives who teach use of their software. With a few phone calls directly to the software companies, you can soon develop a training plan for your personnel.

If you do not have an instructional design and training development staff, then it is likely that you would contract the development of the computer-based training. Appendix A lists some of the vendors who develop computer-based training programs. It is very important that you evaluate completed products that potential contractors have done. Companies may tell you that they are "currently working on a project that will push the envelope and revolutionize training," but you should be far less interested in it than in seeing products that are complete and demonstrate a company's record of delivering on time and on budget. Additionally, carefully look at the instructional systems design aspects of the contractors' products and avoid getting blown away with the glitz of video. Of course, you will want to contact other customers for their references on the ability of potential contractors to produce.

CBT Case Study

EDS has over 95,000 employees worldwide at a multitude of geographic locations. Meeting the training needs of an audience that is so widely dispersed has many inherent challenges. Developing high-quality computer-based training courses has helped EDS to effectively meet many of these training challenges.

"One of the training needs we have is to teach nonfinancial leaders how to interpret financial statements, "explains Gayle Day, lead instructional designer for the development of one of the computer-based training courses. "We had been flying people to central training locations and teaching two-day classroom courses. However, with thousands of employees who needed the course, we knew we needed an alternative delivery medium to reach the training audience." The Accounting and Financial Education team considered several alternatives before deciding to develop a computer-based training course entitled Interpreting Basic Financial

Statements. (Refer to Figure 9 on page 41.) Some of the criteria that were key in their selection of computer-based training were

- ability to distribute it quickly to any place
- ability to distribute it at any time without scheduling constraints
- ability to allow the learner to control flow of instruction
- ability to present training in an interactive performance-based environment
- recognition that instructional content was to remain stable and seldom change.

A team of multimedia developers within the EDS corporate training area took on the project. This multimedia development team takes a metaphor approach when designing computer-based training. For example, the financial statements course uses the metaphor of an 18th century shipping company. To navigate, the learners use their mouse to drag a ship to various "ports" which represent the different subject areas. The computer-based training explains the various financial statements that this shipping company uses. The financial statements are based on a "gold coin" currency system. This allows the course to easily be used in an international training environment rather than basing it on any particular country's currency. Choosing an 18th century period was a very conscious decision because the content has a long shelf life and the historical period ensured that graphics and video elements would not be dated.

Alex Nestor, project leader for another computer-based training course, Systems Life Cycle 3 Overview, elaborates on the use of a metaphor: "It provides an interactive break from the typical tutorial sequence." In the life-cycle course, the learners begin the computer-based training with the screen showing a room where all objects are in black and white. Various objects within the room represent modules within the computer-based training. The students click on the objects and this begins the module of instruction. As they complete the module they are returned to the room and the selected object becomes colorized providing a contrast against the black and white environment. Nestor adds, "We wanted to have a simplified user interface. This room metaphor, or 'discover den' as we call it, provides that interface."

EDS is particularly proud of the response that it is receiving from the field. Each day it receives around 10 requests for the Interpreting Basic Financial Statements CD-ROM. "It's also rewarding to get feedback that non-financial leaders are enthusiastic about learning accounting and financial principals," says Day. The computer-based training courses developed by EDS have also received external recognition. The courses have received awards such as the Macromedia International Users Conference People's Choice Award and the Silver Cindy from the International Association for Audio-Visual Communicators.

In addition to achieving a very high quality of computer-based training, they also developed it in a very cost-effective manner. Though they anticipate training thousands and thousands of personnel through the use of computer-based training, the return on investment is reached long before that time. EDS calculated that when only 800 personnel had completed the financial statements course, it had already paid for itself in cost savings from travel and per diem!

What advice does the EDS team have for those who are considering using computer-based training as a means of delivering training? Day says, "Take the time to have your content written out, sequenced, and designed for online display before you begin." She continued, "Take advantage of the media to reinforce learning by designing and prototyping as many interactions as your budget and schedule will allow. The more learners can 'practice and do' rather than 'read and know' the more engaging and effective the product."

Nestor advises, "Don't use clip-art. It looks like clip-art. However, there are clip-media libraries on CD-ROM that you should consider. There are some excellent digital photos that can be incorporated as well as audio libraries of music and sounds."

They also recommend that organizations considering computer-based training pick a very small project to start. Begin with one or two hours of instruction and learn from the process that you have to go through to accomplish that. Vic Case, administrative manager for the development team, cautions, "Multimedia software companies sometimes make some pretty strong claims in their ads that anyone can use their product and develop good instructional media. If you want to achieve a sophisticated level of interactivity, you will need skilled programmers who understand programming logic. Developing computer-based training can require specialized skills for different medial elements, such as audio or video production." The team highly recommends having someone on the development team who really understands interactivity. This can add a tremendous amount of value to the medium itself.

Computer-based training can be a very effective distance learning tool. By carefully following the lessons learned from other organizations such as EDS, you can add this tool to the selection of media you have to meet the challenges of training in the 21st century.

Authoring computer-based training programs, distributing the product to the field, and familiarizing personnel with how to use it all take time. It is not unusual for this cycle to take 12 to 18 months. Consequently, when considering CBT, you need to be attuned to the likelihood that the subject matter will change. Rapidly fluctuating subjects would not be appropriate content for training material.

The advantages of computer-based training are that they are adaptable to self-paced training, have inexpensive distribution costs, and enable assessment of the learners' comprehension throughout the training. Disadvantages include long production cycles and high authoring costs if course production is done outside the organization.

Computer-Based Training: Distance Learning Technical Summary

Using personal computers and software written to train the learners in a particular subject area. Range from simple, mostly text-based screens to more complex software that includes video, sound, and animation.

Advantages	Disadvantages
Allows self-paced training	High costs for development
Inexpensive distribution costs	Lengthy development timelines
Evaluation built into instruction	Individuals need moderate computer literacy to use
Enables use of existing videos and visuals	

Chapter Seven

Computer Conferencing and Training via the Internet and Intranets

Introduction

Imagine a learner standing at the gates of a large corporate training center or university campus. On the campus are other learners, instructors, reference centers, and various classrooms that will help the individual receive the knowledge, skills, and abilities to perform his job. What he must do is "navigate" from one classroom or building to another to retrieve the appropriate resource material and participate in the appropriate scheduled training sessions.

The Internet and Intranets provide ways for organizations to create an electronic campus that the learner can navigate to interact with other learners, instructors, reference materials, and training sessions. Rather than using tennis shoes, the learner uses his PC to move from one site to another. Unlike the university campus, which is limited to a collection of buildings at one location, the electronic campus may have resources separated by thousands of miles.

A little background might be helpful as you consider whether your organization might use the Internet or an Intranet to deliver training. The Internet began in 1969 as a U.S. Department of Defense experiment connecting four computers to test communication capabilities between computer networks. Since that time, it has grown to more than a million computers linked worldwide. It is estimated that an additional 1,000 computers are added to the Internet each day.

Up until just a few short years ago, accessing information from other computers on the Internet was not a user-friendly process. Although important information was available, it took a high degree of computer and network literacy to know how to get it. With the establishment of the World Wide Web and browser software, the doors to the Internet were suddenly flung open to all who wanted to travel its reaches.

The browser software replaced complicated text commands with easy to use screens that allowed users to point and click their way to the information they wanted. Browsers also allowed users to view photos, graphs, crude quality video, and even sound over the Internet. Information that was previously hidden as computer files with hard to understand names became accessible as Web pages. These pages are graphical documents that display the requested information in an easy-to-read format. Figure 10 on the next page is an example of a Web page as it would appear on a PC screen.

Organizations soon found that they could use the same software and the same computer setup that was working on the Internet and create a network of computers called an Intranet that was accessible only to their authorized employees. The

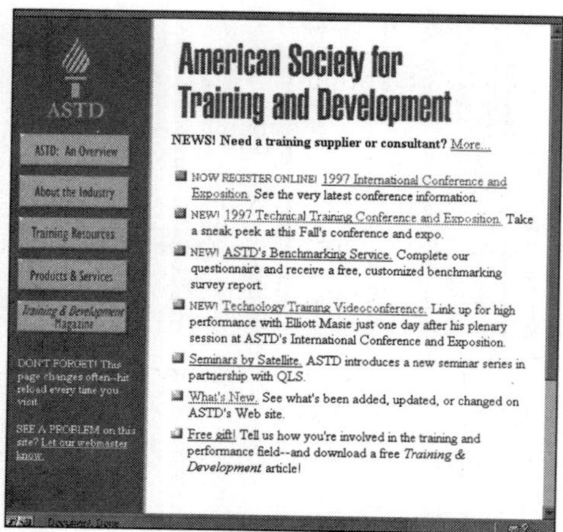

Figure 10. Screen-capture of ASTD Home Page.
This ASTD Web page is available on any PC with Internet access. Courtesy ASTD.

primary use initially was to share information such as project reports, policy manuals, and company databases.

An important difference between an Intranet and the Internet is each one's reach. The Internet has a worldwide scope and can be traveled by anyone having access through a PC and a connection to the Internet. The computers connected to it are intended to be used by external organizations and individuals. The Intranets are usually intended for a restricted audience—those who have authorized access, usually the employees of the organization that owns the Intranet. The Intranet may be connected to the larger Internet so that employees can have access to information from the Internet. However, a firewall, or computer security system, prevents external organizations or individuals from accessing the Intranet.

It did not take long before educators and trainers began to use the Internet and Intranets for instruction and training purposes. Some of the tools that the Internet and Intranet made available to trainers include the following:

Bulletin Board Discussions

Learners and instructors ask a question or make a remark by posting an e-mail message to a bulletin board in much the same way that they would pin a note on a cork board. Everyone in the class can see the message and respond or comment if they feel so inclined.

Direct E-mail Communication

Learners send e-mail to the instructor or another learner individually to seek assistance or comment on some aspect of the training.

Online Course and Reference Materials

Rather than distribute paper copies of course texts, practical exercises, case studies, or other reference materials, the trainer posts the documents to the Net (abbreviation for both the Internet and Intranet), and learners can access them directly. Of course, learners can always print out a hard copy if they prefer.

Live Computer Conferencing

An instructor can set up a live conference room or chat room for all the class members to log into at the same time. Anything a learner types on his or her PC is displayed on the screen for all to see along with that learner's name. Figure 11 on the next page is an example of an online computer conference session. As you can imagine, this type of conference could become a mixture of disconnected sentences and thoughts if uncontrolled. Protocols are established to facilitate the orderly flow of discussion. The discussion text can also be stored so that participants can later review it.

At the present time, print, graphs, and still photos can be distributed over the Internet or Intranet rather easily. Video and sound are not easily distributed. The amount of information that has to travel to deliver a high-quality 60-second video clip chokes the capacity of the computer network and ends up looking like an early Charlie Chaplan film. Rapid advances are being made in this area however and may soon allow trainers to use the Nets for transmission of training videos as well.

Your organization or company may already have an established local area network (LAN) or wide area network (WAN) that connects the various computers and PCs. In addition to that, what is needed to use this existing asset for training purposes? The instructor and each learner will need to have access to a PC that has an Internet or Intranet connection. The PC will need to have Web browser software installed. Appendix A lists some of the currently used browsers. Of course, you will want to provide training to the personnel on the software. One of the advantages of using the Internet or Intranet is that once you have trained personnel on the use of the browser, that same software can be used to participate in and access several different training courses.

Those readers without an organizational network can turn to a commercial provider for these services. Several online services provide space on dial-in computer networks as well as the necessary development expertise if needed.

****From Carol:**	We consider our accreditation evaluations as level 4.
****From Mike:**	We've just begun level 3 and are looking at level 4. Hence my interest here.
****From Edith:**	Mike, how are you conducting level 3?
****From Mike:**	Currently we are conducting field on-the-job observations.
****From Ted:**	Mike, is the role strictly observation, or do you get participant feedback?
****From Richard:**	Job observations? Are your workers union or non?
****From Mike:**	I believe it has been strictly observation. We are in the middle of them now. These are union employees.
****From Carol:**	Our foremen, supervisors, and managers perform job observations. Our peers and management perform training observations.
****From Carol:**	Our trainers perform written or face-to-face post training surveys and interviews.
****From Mike:**	Our job observations are used to determine if our training has been used in practice. These are done by the trainers.
****From Ted:**	Butch, are there problems coordinating all that info from various sources?
****From Edith:**	Mike, who sees the results of the observations? Who uses the feedback?
****From Richard:**	My boss is now asking for a "cost-benefit analysis" that ties into our mission state ment every time I conduct training or spend much money? Any ideas on how to put one together?

Figure 11. Live Computer Conference Transcript.
A live computer conference transcript displays whatever participants type along with their names. Courtesy ASTD.

You will also need someone to prepare the Web pages and maintain the electronic training site. This person is often referred to as the Webmaster. The same browser software that allows your learners to view the Internet or Intranet can be used to publish the Web pages that contain the course texts and varied reference material. Depending on your organization, you may choose to have someone receive the appropriate training to do this, or you may contract or outsource the creation of these Web pages.

Training courses that are largely text-based or self-paced are ideal candidates for delivery via the Internet or Intranet. Advantages of Internet- and Intranet-based training are that learners can access the materials from anywhere as long as they have Internet or Intranet connectivity. The cost of training delivery is already covered by the existing infrastructure required to establish the computer network. Materials can be easily modified or updated, and once users are trained with browser software, they can use the same software for various courses. Disadvantages of Internet- and Intranet-based training include the level of expertise needed to create training Web sites, limitations on transmission of video or sound, and security measures needed to prevent external use of a training site.

Internet Training Case Study

Think for a moment about providing training to hundreds of thousands of people employed by the federal government. Remember that this audience is dispersed in each of the United States as well as internationally. Now add to that challenge, far-reaching legislation that requires specific performance measures from federally supported agencies within a fairly short period of time to retain funding. How would you approach this seemingly insurmountable task?

David Lamp and members of the United States Department of Agriculture Rural Internet Training Environment (RITE) project set out not only to meet this training requirement for their agency, but also to provide a tool that would allow other agencies to easily use the Internet as a training vehicle.

The project was initiated as a result of mandated performance measures enacted by the Government Performance and Results Act (GPRA). This legislation required agencies to institute a results-based management approach. Future federal funding would be dependent on demonstrated performance. In other words, you had to prove what you do with funds that you receive. The state of Oregon was singled out by the President and his Cabinet as a model to follow in instituting results-based management. Lamp and the RITE team began to build a training tool that would make accessible on the Internet information on what Oregon had done to achieve its level of performance.

In choosing the Internet as the training vehicle and creating a tool for trainers, the RITE team considered several criteria, including the following:

- essentially unlimited distribution capability
- ready access throughout the nation including rural communities
- low costs
- easy adaptability to others' training requirements.

The RITE tool is a piece of software loaded on the local PC that automates the creation of Internet Web pages that will be used for training others. The software acts as an instructional design assistant for trainers, policy makers, and GPRA implementers. It asks for basic information about the subject to be presented, such as the following:

- What are the objectives of the training or presentation?
- What modules make up the topic?
- What tasks make up the module?
- What information is presented in each task?

Based on a user's responses, the software then generates Web pages that can be loaded onto the Internet. The implications are significant. All who access the Web pages will view a standardized presentation of the subject matter. This avoids information being left out by a well-meaning trainer who may have felt that a particular topic was not necessary. Everybody gets the same message! This is especially important for legally mandated training.

Those involved in the RITE project are using this software tool to get the word out, provide training on GPRA compliance requirements, and share information on models of achievement such as Oregon.

To access the training that is being put on the Internet through the use of this tool, the requirements are fairly simple. Users need a personal computer, a modem, and access to the Internet. This access can be provided by companies such as CompuServe, America Online, or local service providers. The learner then uses the computer and modem to dial over a regular phone line into the Internet. Once connected, the learner goes to the address of the pages created by the RITE project software.

Lamp says the team is proud that it is providing a tool that breaks down some of the earlier barriers to using the Internet for training. Prior to the development of the RITE tool, developing Web pages for training via the Internet was restricted to those who knew how to write HTML codes (HyperText Markup Language, the computer programming language that is used for Internet web pages) or those who had a friend in the computer department. The RITE project changes that and puts the capability in the hands of trainers and managers.

What advice would the RITE team give to others considering using the Internet as a training medium? Remember to change your mindset as you develop Internet training. "In a residential training environment," Lamp explains, "the teacher is the one with the power. They stand in front of the class, they have the books, they have the schedule, etc. With Internet training, the learners have a choice. They can get rid of you as a teacher with one mouse click." Lamp suggests a model where you create curiosity, present a problem, and then provide a solution.

With the merging of telecommunication companies, cable providers, and software companies, you can anticipate that the number of your employees that have Internet access at home as well as work will dramatically increase within the next few years. This creates a new concept when we think of where our training classrooms are. With tools such as the RITE software, you will be able to use the Internet to reach into those classrooms and provide learners with a multitude of training opportunities.

Internet and Intranet-Based Training: Distance Learning Technical Summary

A network of linked computers allows learners and instructors to interact using e-mail, online computer conferencing, and e-mail message boards. Course and reference materials are made available online for learners to view or download.

Advantages	Disadvantages
Materials readily updated	Moderate to high degree of computer literacy to create Web training sites
Inexpensive distribution costs	Video and sound transmission extremely limited
Access to multiple courses with training on single piece of Web software	Security measures to prevent unwanted viewing
Self-paced training	

Selecting Appropriate Technologies

INTRODUCTION

Now that we have looked at some of the distance learning technologies, you are probably wondering which one to use for your training requirements. Refer to the introduction to this section. The answer to the question is, "All of them!" Depending on what it is that you are training, one technology may be preferable to another or several of the media could be used equally well to train learners in the task. How do you know which one to use, and is there a process that can help you to choose? In the previous chapters in this section, we have considered what the technologies are and what you need to use them. In this chapter, we will look at what these technologies mean for a trainer who has to provide training in specific tasks and how that trainer should use the technologies. These steps are often referred to as the media selection process.

It will be helpful to set aside for a moment the way we have always trained. Instead of focusing on different training or instructional techniques that have been used, focus on the performance objective. It is important to have a clear idea of what you want the learner to be able to do at the end of training for a particular task. Will the learner be required to demonstrate some action? Is performance limited to recitation of facts or figures? Does correct performance consist of primarily filling out forms without error? Clearly establish what it is that you expect at the conclusion of training a task.

Now that you have established or reiterated a clear learning objective for the task, let's ask a series of questions that will help to decide which distance learning technology would be appropriate. Refer to the matrix on the next page. If the answer to the question in column one is yes, then any of the media that have an X in their columns could be appropriate choices for training in the task. By continuing down the list of questions in column one, you can quickly decide which media would be appropriate.

Pick some of the tasks or learning objectives that are part of your current courses. Practice using the matrix to determine appropriate media that might be used. Now with the understanding that you have gained earlier in this section, try to visualize a training session being conducted using that particular technology. Soon you will be able to think in terms of the strengths, weaknesses, and capabilities of each of the technologies as you develop training events and courses.

In this section, we have reviewed the technologies or tools needed for effective distance learning. We have also looked at how you select the appropriate tool based on the task that you are going to train or teach. You now have a solid foundation and conceptual framework that will greatly enhance your ability to understand many of the other issues associated with distance learning. Experiencing the technologies in use will amplify your current understanding. In the next section, we will explain how you can easily experiment with and test the varied distance learning tools. This will help you progress even further on your road to dramatically improving your ability to train, teach, and reach your target audience.

Media Selection Matrix

If the answer to the question in the first column is yes, then the media with an "X" in its column could be an appropriate choice for the training task. By continuing down the list of questions in the first column, you can quickly decide which media would be appropriate.

	Self-Paced Instruction					Live Interactive Instruction				
	Print	Audiotape	Videotape	Computer-Based Training	Internet/ Intranet	Computer Conferencing	Audio Teletraining	Audio-Graphics	ITV	VTC
Is live interaction between the instructor and student required to teach the task?						X	X	X	X	X
Will the use of motion video enhance the learning objective?			X	X					X	X
If live interactive motion is required, will the course be offered on a continuous basis to a large number of sites?									X	
If live interactive motion is required, will the course be offered to a small number of sites that will need to be visible to each other?										X
Do I need to observe the student performing an action?										X
Is the course or training primarily based on print materials?	X			X	X					
Does the material change frequently?	X				X	X	X	X		
* Is special equipment or materials required to train the task?										
* Do students need extensive interaction—both visual and audio—with each other?										

*These cases require special case-by-case consideration. Residential training may be preferred. A careful analysis of the performance objectives will help you in this process.

Experiencing It

Imagine sitting down to put together a large jigsaw puzzle. You spread out hundreds of pieces on the table. What would it be like to proceed without having a picture of the completed puzzle to refer to? Some of the individual pieces would be recognizable as part of a tree or pieces of brick, but you would be at a definite disadvantage when trying to fit the pieces together into a beautiful finished product.

This section of the book will help provide you with the steps necessary for the completed picture of distance learning. Without that perspective, the relationship among the technology, instructors, course content, and learners may seem very confusing, and the various pieces that go into developing and designing your own distance learning program may seem disjointed. With an appropriate frame of reference, however, the pieces become an effective training system.

In our work with several organizations in new distance learning initiatives, we are often asked, "Is there some way that we can experience distance learning before we create our own program?" We have found it invaluable to have key personnel participate in distance learning events at the very outset of the effort. These early experiences provide some reference points as the organization moves forward in establishing its own distance learning program.

Before you experience the distance learning events recommended in this section, prepare a checklist of questions to ask yourself as you participate. Your checklist may include items like the following:

- How does this apply to my organization?
- What do I like about the way this information is being presented?
- Which of our instructors would be likely candidates for teaching this way?
- How did the presenter handle the interaction with the learners?
- How did learners ask questions?
- How did the instructor call on learners?
- How long did the training take?
- What would I change?
- What were the costs associated with the training?
- What medium was used to deliver the training?
- How do I feel about participating?

These questions are just a start. Use this list or create your own list and take it with you to your first few events.

Experience It as a Learner

INTRODUCTION

What is it like to be on the receiving end of a distance learning event? Dozens of live interactive distance learning events will be going on around you this month. One of the first steps in experiencing an event is to be a participant—a learner.

In the previous chapter, we discussed interactive television, currently the most widely used distance learning technology. Now you have the opportunity to experience it as a learner. Appendix B lists some of the key corporations, federal agencies, and academic institutions that have active distance learning programs. Review that list. Is there a corporation or agency that is similar to yours? Contact several of those listed and ask for a schedule of upcoming distance learning events. Some of the events may require a registration fee. Many of the federal agencies will allow you to participate at no cost.

The U.S. Postal Service has one of the most active federal distance learning programs. It also has the largest number of downlink or learner distance learning facilities in the federal government. This means that if you are in a major metropolitan area, there is a good chance that the post office mail-processing center in your city has a distance learning classroom. A phone call can confirm that. Ask to speak with the training officer. We have found that with advance notice, many of the locations are willing to showcase their excellent distance learning program.

On the corporate side, the Ford Motor Company has installed 6,000 distance learning classrooms nationwide. These training classrooms are located at dealerships. Again, a phone call can determine whether there is one in your local area or not. The name of the distance learning network is called FordStar Training Network. The dealerships we have contacted have been proud of their classrooms and invited us to see them. (Rick Gividen was asked if he was considering buying a new car!)

When you visit, be sure to bring with you the checklist of questions that we described in the introduction to this section. Then enjoy the experience. Pay particular attention to your feelings as a learner. Is the material clearly presented? Do you feel a part of the class or like an outside observer?

COMPUTER-BASED INSTRUCTION

Sometime this month schedule an hour to go to your local computer superstore. Budget $75 for the experience. Browse through the educational and training CD-ROM software. Find a product that may apply to your organization's training needs or simply one that sounds like fun. What is something you have wanted to learn how to do? Is there a language that you have wanted to learn? Perhaps you have needed a primer on home repair or auto mechanics. The list of topics covered by commercial computer-based training products grows each day.

Select one and take it to your office or home to evaluate. Pull out your checklist of questions. In this case, the instructor is the CD-ROM. Consider not only the bells and whistles of the software but the instructional design aspects as well. How well does the program adapt to different levels of learner capabilities? How is your performance evaluated as you go through the program?

Your completed checklist of questions from the interactive television event and the CD-ROM experience has prepared you for the next step: experiencing it as a trainer!

CHAPTER TEN

Experience It as a Trainer

INTRODUCTION

I don't see how distance learning would work for what I teach. I depend on a lot of nonverbal communication from the learners. You know, the "I don't get it look."

What happens if everybody wants to ask a question at once from all of the remote sites? How could you possibly handle that chaos?

How do you monitor the learners at the remote sites to make sure they are paying attention?

I use the white board a lot in my class. How could I do that with distance learning?

These are common questions from trainers and instructors who are being introduced to distance learning. Hesitancy, uncertainty, resistance, and defensiveness are all fairly normal reactions when a trainer is first approached about teaching at a distance. Usually these reactions come from a genuine concern for learners and the trainer's pride in ensuring that the learners learn the course material. The trainer is unsure that distance learning will provide learners with the same learning opportunity as residential instruction. Be assured that by giving those trainers an opportunity for firsthand experience with some experiments or pilots, the uncertainty will give way to confidence in distance learning as a training tool.

Think back to our analogy of the jigsaw puzzle at the beginning of this section. If trainers or instructors have never experienced teaching at a distance, what picture would they use to form a concept of how the class will go? That's right. The tendency would be to compare it to the same style of training they have been using in the traditional classroom setting. It is like a lumberjack who has used a handsaw all of his life looking at a chain saw and trying to imagine how to push it back and forth to saw a tree in half manually.

PREPARE THE TRAINERS

Before conducting pilot events, it is important to prepare the trainers. One way is to have the trainers contact one of the organizations listed in Appendix B and visit with instructors who are already training at a distance. Some questions to ask might include the following:

- How did they feel about training at a distance the first time?
- What did they do to encourage interaction from the learners?
- How did they adapt course materials that were used in the classroom?

- What have they changed as they have become more experienced at training at a distance?

- What technical difficulties have they experienced with the technology, and how did they handle them?

It is highly recommended that the trainers observe an actual distance learning event at the organization they are visiting.

A second option for preparing the trainers is to take a course specifically designed to prepare instructors to teach at a distance. These courses are offered from commercial sources as well as from government sources for those trainers within federal or state agencies. Appendix A contains a partial list of training resources.

Audio Teletraining Pilot

One of the simplest pilots can be done using audio teletraining. This pilot can help trainers take that first step outside of the traditional classroom. To conduct the initial audio teletraining pilot, you need

- two audio teletraining conveners (see Chapter Three)
- a classroom with a standard telephone jack
- an instructor room or office with a standard telephone jack
- an instructor
- three to six "learners" (can be staff or actual trainees)
- a one- to two-hour block of instruction or training material.

We recommend that you pick a block of instruction that already has some excellent support materials. Is there a segment that you train that has some learner workbooks, practical exercises, or other prepared aids? This would be a likely candidate for the initial pilot.

After selecting the block of instruction, select a trainer and learners. The trainer should have been previously trained in distance learning techniques, as described above. The learners may be actual trainees who need the block of instruction or staff who do not necessarily need the instruction but are helping in the distance learning initiative.

Establish early on how you will evaluate the learners' achievement of the learning objectives. Perhaps there is already a test or evaluation instrument in place for the block of instruction. If so, this step would be fairly easy. If not, consider developing one so performance can be measured. The evaluation instrument helps to build confidence in the distance learning initiative. It provides an objective measure that helps all involved to understand that the learners taught at a distance can perform as well or better than those taught in a residential setting.

With the trainer prepared, block of instruction selected, and learners identified, the next step is to train the learners. Set one convener up in the classroom with the learners. Set the other convener up in the trainer's office or another classroom. You may also want to set up a tape recorder or camcorder to record the event for later review. Now conduct the training session. The first few minutes may be somewhat awkward as the trainer and trainees step outside of the comfort zone of the traditional classroom setting, but their focus will soon shift to the subject matter and to ensuring that the learners understand the material. As this change happens, the technology will become transparent and the "classroom" will become the learning experience.

The pilot ends with administration of an objective evaluation instrument. It is helpful to get all of those involved to discuss their perceptions of the training event. You will undoubtedly get comments such as, "I would have rather been in the classroom with the instructor" or "I think it would have been better if we could have seen the instructor." These are normal reactions and responses, even when the learners outperform their resident counterparts on the objective evaluation. What learners prefer and what helps them best achieve the learning objectives are not necessarily one and the same.

The next step would be for your organization to conduct the same block of instruction, except at a number of remote sites (two to 10 are recommended for an initial event) and for trainees who need that instruction. The additional equipment needed would be a convener for each site and the use of an audio bridge. Refer to Appendix A for a list of bridging service providers. You are now on your way to implementing audio teletraining as one of your distance learning tools.

Interactive Television Pilot

An interactive television pilot requires considerably more preparation than the audio teletraining event previously described. However, the results that can be achieved even with one pilot of an interactive television event can dramatically enhance the effectiveness of training. The Army National Guard carefully planned its first interactive television pilot. By following a planning template similar to the one you will see in the next chapter, the Guard was able to provide training to more than 2,400 soldiers in two days. The pilot event became a regularly offered training course that is conducted several times each year.

The importance of preparing instructors for an interactive television event cannot be overemphasized. An effective event consists of much more than standing in front of a camera. Organizations are strongly encouraged to benchmark with similar organizations that are already training at a distance. The adage "It is better to learn from the mistakes of others" certainly applies here. The instructors who volunteer or are volunteered for the initial pilot events deserve every opportunity to succeed. Preparation is part of that opportunity. (See Chapter Nineteen.)

An interactive television pilot will provide the organization with a multitude of opportunities and learning experiences. It requires a cooperative effort by those providing the training and those at the remote sites who will be receiving the training. The following chapter describes a step-by-step planning template to assist in the conduct of interactive television events. Planners who study the template and adapt it to their particular situation at an organization can confidently move forward and conduct a pilot event that will not only provide necessary training but will also help them progress toward full implementation of a distance learning program.

CHAPTER ELEVEN

Experience It as a Manager

INTRODUCTION

An effective and successful distance learning event requires detailed planning. It is a team effort that requires cross-functional coordination among organizational departments. The project manager for a distance learning course or event must bring together various organizational resources and track the different steps along the way to keep an event on schedule. We have developed a template that has helped many project managers with their first interactive television event. It also serves as a checklist while planning training events.

A short series of questions can help a trainer focus on what event would be appropriate for the first interactive television pilot. The questions are

- Who are the members of your training audience?
- If you could get all of them together in an auditorium for one to four hours, what training or information would you cover with them?
- What training or information would they want?

The answers to these questions will help you plan on a short event that will have a positive impact on your training audience. By using the planning template, you will be able to successfully conduct that event within six months and reach a large portion of your training audience. The last question we usually ask is, "If you do not conduct the pilot event, will you be able to get this vital training to the training audience? If you will, what percentage of your training audience will receive it?"

Having identified a critical one- to four-hour block of instruction, you are now ready to use the planning template. The template is divided into seven major areas. (See Section Five for in-depth coverage of these areas.) The areas are

- course development
- instructor training
- instructor site preparation
- remote site preparation
- course administration and registration
- training event implementation
- project review meetings.

Review the Pilot Event Management Template at the end of this chapter. It shows suggested lead times for accomplishing each activity. The template is driven by the date on which you will conduct the event. Fill in the date of the event at the top of the template. Now refer to the "Start Action" column and the "Action Completed Date" columns. Fill in dates in the "Start Action" column based on your selected event date and the recommended number of days lead time from the "Begin the task" column.

Now go down the "DL Team Member Responsible" column and tentatively pencil in which team member you think should be responsible for that action. This is where you will gain experience that can only come from planning and conducting a distance learning event. Some of the traditional roles of trainers, technical support, or information managers begin to blend in a distance learning event. It is suggested that you form a team with representatives from each of the departments that have a role in the pilot. The team can then discuss those areas that may be a little gray.

At the conclusion of this exercise, you will have a completed template that you can use to help you conduct your event. You are ready to get your distance learning team together and start down the road to having one distance learning event under your belt!

Experience It! Case Study

Chief Warrant Officer Eddie Glover is an instructor at the Army National Guard Professional Education Center. The center has been a traditional residential training schoolhouse since 1974. Glover has taught a three-week residential course for unit personnel clerks since 1985. The technical, skills-based course trains the clerks to perform a myriad of administrative tasks required in their daily jobs.

The center began to research implementation of a distance learning program and selected Glover's course as a potential candidate for distance learning by audio teletraining. When approached, Glover was polite, but resistant: "I don't see how we could do this course if I can't see the learners and they can't see me."

He went on to express other concerns: "There is a lot of interaction in my classroom. I can tell a lot about whether the learners are getting the information by looking at their body language. Sometimes their eyes glaze over and I can tell I need to adjust my instruction.

"I also use the whiteboard a lot in my course," he continued. "I'm not sure I can teach to the same standard without the whiteboard."

Glover agreed to observe audio teletraining at the U.S. Postal Service's Technical Training Center in Norman, Oklahoma ("Experience It as a Learner!") and then decide whether he would do a pilot event. The visit to that center helped him to understand how distance learning does not mean less contact with the learners. He observed instructors and learners in lively interaction. It was obvious they were grasping the course content. He came away from the visit saying, "This *might* be able to work."

Shortly after the visit to the Technical Training Center, Glover decided to conduct his own experiment. He took a new instructor, who was unfamiliar with the tasks he taught, and designated her as the learner. Glover sat in a building on one side of the campus while she was in a building on the other side. Using audio teletraining equipment, he taught her a task and then gave her the same evaluation used in the residential course. She passed. This was a turning point in his acceptance of distance learning as a training tool. He was "experiencing it as a trainer."

After disclosing the results of his own experiment, Glover told the distance learning project officer, "I think the pilot event will work."

The pilot was conducted with 24 learners at 10 sites around the nation. The learners had a higher pass rate than the residential learners on all task evaluations! Glover now teaches the entire clerk course via audio teletraining. The center saves $50,000 in travel and per diem costs for each course conducted through distance learning.

The turning point in Glover's acceptance was Experiencing It!

Pilot Event Management Template

	Distance Learning Team Member Responsible	Start Action Date	Action Completed Date	Begin the task This many days prior to the event	Complete the task This many days prior to the event
Course Development					
Identify your training audience for event.	________	________	________	120	100
Determine event objective.	________	________	________	100	95
Use existing or create new training lesson plan.	________	________	________	90	85
Identify visual aids needed.	________	________	________	85	80
Create or obtain visual aids.	________	________	________	85	45
Create or modify course evaluation instrument.	________	________	________	85	75
Create remote site support packet.	________	________	________	85	75
Hold first rehearsal on mock audience.	________	________	________	40	35
Fine-tune to course materials.	________	________	________	30	20
Have final rehearsal.	________	________	________	10	20
Instructor Training					
Select primary and alternate instructors.	________	________	________	95	90
Train instructors on teaching at a distance.	________	________	________	70	40
Hold instructor site orientation.	________	________	________	40	20
Hold first rehearsal on mock audience.	________	________	________	40	35
Have final rehearsal.	________	________	________	10	20
Instructor Site Preparation					
Identify possible instructor sites.	________	________	________	85	80
Select instructor sites.	________	________	________	80	75
Contract for use of instructor sites.	________	________	________	75	70
Hold instructor site orientation.	________	________	________	40	20
Travel to instructor sites.	________	________	________	2	

Pilot Event Management Template (continued)

	Distance Learning Team Member Responsible	Start Action Date	Action Completed Date	Begin the task This many days prior to the event	Complete the task
Remote Site Preparation					
Identify remote sites that will participate.	______	______	______	70	65
Contract for use of remote sites.	______	______	______	75	70
Identify remote site facilitators.	______	______	______	55	45
Hold audio conference with remote site facilitators.	______	______	______	45	0
Prepare remote site.	______	______	______	at least one hour before event	
Course Administration and Registration					
Market class to training audience.	______	______	______	75	20
Identify remote site facilitators.	______	______	______	55	45
Generate employee attendee list.	______	______	______	20	
Mail remote site packets.	______	______	______	15	
Create master list of actual attendees.	______	______	______		
Collect all evaluations.	______	______	______		
The Training Event					
Establish connectivity.	______	______	______	30-60 minutes before event	
Send test pattern.	______	______	______	30-60 minutes before event	
Conduct course.	______	______	______		
Conduct course evaluation.	______	______	______	within 15 days	
Analyze course evaluations.	______	______	______		
Project Review Meetings					
Initial concept review.	______	______	______	120	
Meeting 1.	______	______	______	90	
Meeting 2.	______	______	______	60	
Meeting 3.	______	______	______	30	
Final project review meeting.	______	______	______	15	
Post-event review meeting (after analysis of course evaluations).	______	______	______		

Justifying the Need for Distance Learning

Now that you've had the opportunity to see the features, advantages, and benefits of different distance learning methods of delivery, you are ready to prepare and present the justification for establishing distance learning in your organization. Selling the concept of distance learning is easy, but getting the money for it may not be. To be successful in getting the funds, you must have a strategic plan in which you link the distance learning program directly to the bottom line and justify the necessary expenditures. Not so easy to do, but it has been done successfully time and time again with a strong cost-justification process.

To prepare your strategic plan, consider your needs assessment. Do the course requirements and needs of the learners require learning outcomes that can best be delivered by one of the following methods?

- computer-based training
- Internet or Intranet
- CD-ROM
- diskettes
- two-way video, two-way audio
- desktop videoconferencing
- satellite one-way video, two-way audio
- audio teleconferencing
- audiographics.

You must detail in your strategic plan each of the options you select. This chapter will help guide you toward getting the money you need for each phase of your distance learning plan. Are you asking for everything for the next five years? Do you want just one or two options? Whatever you choose, this chapter will help explain the key areas to focus on as you seek approval for your distance learning requests. Naturally, as you work in a bottom-line mindset, you must justify every investment. This section of the book will provide a model for you to use whenever you need the dollars to meet the learning objectives of your workforce.

We will give you guidelines on what to do and how to do it. We have worked with many organizations in preparing the necessary research and documentation for getting appropriate funding for distance learning initiatives. Many times, funding requests have to be made to individuals who have little or no knowledge of distance learning. Why should they invest in something they know little about when continuous requests for capital equipment and improvement are more easily understood and appear to have a less risky application of precious dollars?

With the incredible amount of details, functional requirements, and dollar requests submitted within an organization, your requests may be received initially as just another one to add to the already overflowing budget in-basket. The key is to ensure that you position distance learning as a strategic, competitive advantage that will enable you and others in your organization to effectively train your geographically dispersed workforce and help seize rapidly changing market opportunities.

Chapter Twelve

Key Elements of Preparation

Introduction

We will identify and discuss the key elements of preparation necessary to produce an effective cost-benefit analysis, including the following:

- identifying the scope of your organization
- defining your current business climate
- developing a distance learning mission statement
- defining distance learning
- identifying and defining different methods of distance learning options
- analyzing current course needs and requirements
- selecting possible courses for distance learning delivery
- identifying your current training output
- analyzing costs associated with travel and lost productivity
- assessing the alternatives available to your organization.

Before we begin to detail these 10 areas, it is important to strengthen your bottom-line thinking. Consider the following conceptual and insightful questions:

First, why should the decision makers listen to your request? All decision makers want to achieve continuous increased profitability. Any initiatives must be positioned in terms of their profitable value to the organization's dealings with the workforce, customer base, and market share. Your beginning positioning statements should include carefully structured wording to capture the readers' interest by tying your distance learning recommendations to the bottom-line.

Second, what's in it for the organization if you have distance learning options? Your request should highlight how distance learning enables the organization to achieve the following:

- save money on training costs for travel

- increase productivity with less time away from the workplace due to training travel requirements

- train more people, more often, with reduced costs

- strengthen your competitive advantage by having cost-effective access to experts around the world

- quickly provide training on new products and services

- quickly address or provide information and solutions to any problems affecting the workforce or its work environment.

Now we are ready to identify the key components of your cost-benefit analysis. Your carefully prepared document will show the key stakeholders how to save money spent on travel, identify the costs of lost productivity due to travel, and document real-world financial justification for your distance learning funding requests.

Identifying the Scope of Your Organization

This positioning statement provides the macro-overview of the size and location of your workforce. You can include current information as well as any plans for targeted strategic growth, such as the addition of new offices or geographic coverage. You should be sure to include the number of employees; geographic boundaries; number of regions, districts, divisions, and the like; and the number of sites. You might say, for example, ABC Corporation has 5,000 employees working in the United States, Europe, and Asia. We have five regions and 35 divisions in those geographic areas. All of our employees work in a regional or divisional office. An additional 200 sites will be added due to new telecommuting arrangements with selected employees.

Defining Your Current Business Environment

Here's where you have the opportunity to state bottom-line facts that will have an impact on the way you need to do business. Because of your corporate environment, you must find new ways not only to do business but also to ensure that conducting business meets both your training needs and the financial parameters established by your organization. You might list such impending events or circumstances affecting your organization as rightsizing, reorganization, retraining for new skills, decreased training budgets, or decreased travel budgets. Also list all of your macro training goals, such as

- reducing travel time and cost for training
- developing a menu-based approach for training delivery options
- increasing productivity with reduced travel and increased training opportunities
- delivering mandated training to the workforce in a consistent and cost-effective manner
- delivering training to employees when and where they need it.

Developing a Distance Learning Mission Statement

Your mission statement should parallel in concept the mission statement for your organization, but it should be training specific. Start with reviewing the company's mission statement and then begin formulating the one for distance learning. An example of a distance learning mission statement could be

> MISSION STATEMENT
>
> The [name of your organization] will provide superior quality, cost-effective, and responsive training and education programs to help our geographically dispersed workforce achieve the highest quality of proficiency and productivity, which will help our workforce achieve professional

> growth and will strengthen our organization. We will utilize the latest proven technologies to provide training when and where the workforce needs it with reduced dependence on travel by our workforce for its training. We will offer the most cost-effective methods of distance learning training delivery while maximizing both the quality and effectiveness of courses offered by [name of organization].

Defining Distance Learning

There are so many different perceived definitions of distance learning that it is important to use the one that will cover all of the bases. We prefer to use the definition from "Guiding Principles for Distance Learning in a Learning Society" by the Center for Adult Learning and Educational Credentials of the American Council on Education.

> Distance learning is a system and a process that connects learners with distributed learning resources. While distance learning takes a wide variety of forms, all distance learning is characterized by
>
> - separation of place and/or time between instructor and learner, among learners, and/or between learners and learning resources
>
> - interaction between the learner and the instructor, among learners and/or between learners and learning resources conducted through one or more media; use of electronic media is not necessarily required.
>
> The learner is an individual or group that seeks a learning experience offered by a provider. The provider is the organization that creates and facilitates the learning opportunity. Providers include schools, colleges and universities, business and industry, professional organizations, labor unions, government agencies, the military and other public and private organizations.

Another simple definition you may hear is "structured learning without the physical presence of an instructor." It is important to clearly state the definition in your cost-justification document. The definition should be easy to understood and broad enough in scope that it covers both existing methods of distance learning delivery as well as those not yet developed. (With the rate of technological change, new technologies will be continuously developed so you don't want to back yourself in a corner with a detailed description.)

Identifying and Defining Methods of Distance Learning Options

You want to structure a visually centered "look" at distance learning methods of delivery. You want to list different options, such as

- video teleconferencing: two-way video, two-way audio
- interactive video teletraining: one-way video, two-way audio

- audio teleconferencing: audio telephone communication
- audiographics: audio telephone communication with graphics on a PC
- computer-based training: CD-ROM, diskettes, Internet, Intranet
- print: hard copy of course material.

Be sure to explain that different methods of distance learning delivery are selected based on the needs and requirements of the course subject and the content and needs of the learners. For example, classified information training may require visual communications, so video teleconferencing may be the best method of distance learning delivery. In your plan, you will want to stress the cardinal rule that applications precede technology to ensure that as your training needs change, you will have the flexibility to add different methods of delivery.

Analyzing Current Course Needs and Requirements

If you have completed a recent needs assessment, you are one step ahead in the distance learning process. A complete curriculum overview to include multilevel training requirements and needs (to cover the workforce from front-line employees to senior management) was the first important step you took as you started on your distance learning journey. With that major step completed, you are in the best possible position to make sound recommendations for new ways to deliver training.

You will base your distance learning delivery decisions on factors such as the identification of the following:

- content to be learned
- applications of the skills and content
- individual or group collaborative needs, or both
- auditory, sensory, and application requirements
- level of trainer-led instruction needed
- level of participation required for learning and application.

Now, you can begin to select the method or methods of delivery that would best support the needs of your multilevel workforce. Section Two provided a picture of the advantages and disadvantages of each distance learning option in your training toolbox. You based your decisions about the best delivery methods on a sound assessment and working knowledge of the different distance learning options described there. The pie chart on the next page shows how a total distance learning delivery system could be broken down.

In preparing this part of your justification documentation, be sure to identify each method of delivery that you have chosen and for each training method describe its cost-savings benefits and its benefits to your organization or the learners, or both. (The basic benefits of each method are listed in Section Two.)

Selecting Possible Courses for Distance Learning Delivery

As you prepare your cost-benefit document, you will identify potential courses that can be transitioned to distance learning delivery. In many organizations, the number of courses taught may make this task seem overwhelming at first. How do

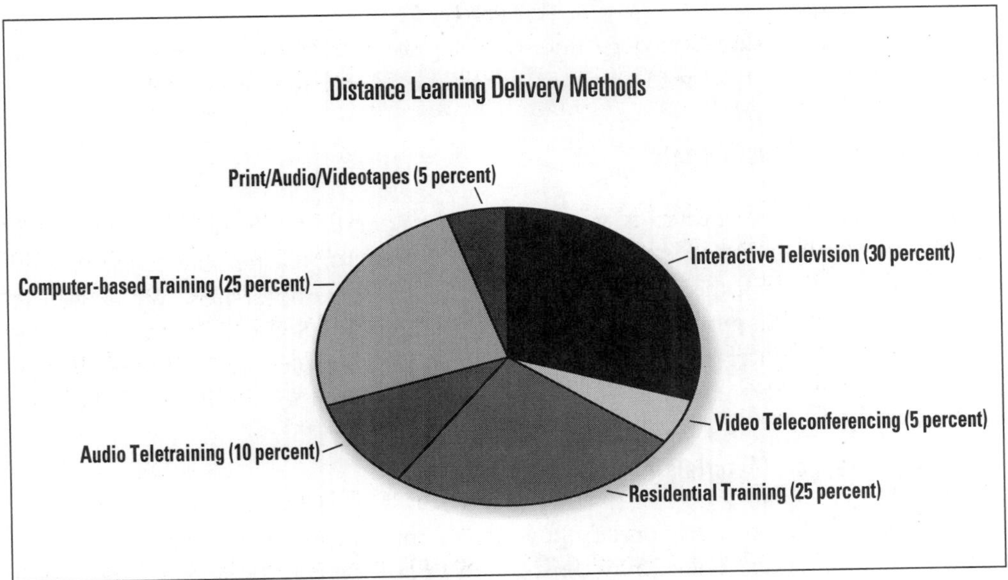

you know which ones can be successfully taught via distance learning. Have faith! There are some key factors to consider that will assist you in this identification process. These include the following:

Annual Course Attendance

What is the total potential audience for this course? How many learners complete the course each year? The return on investment for transitioning a course to distance learning delivery will depend on the anticipated number of learners who will receive the training. Obviously, the greater the number of learners the greater the potential cost avoidance. Remember to consider whether the current number of learners is constrained by variables such as travel costs. You may project that a greater number of learners will complete the course if it is made locally accessible. Courses that have a large backlog of students are prime candidates.

Length of the Course

A two-day course will be easier to transition than a nine-month course. Some professional and career development programs last for several months. The course length in and of itself does not necessarily become an excluding factor. For example, many graduate degree programs are offered entirely at a distance and may take two to three years to complete. However, in most cases your quickest return will be found on those courses that last a few days or a few weeks.

Format of Instruction

What method of instruction is currently used to teach the course? Does it involve lecture, group discussion, role play, practical exercises, case studies or hands on equipment training? Lecture lends it self to a fairly simple transition. Evaluating and discussing a case study can also be transitioned easily. Some role playing situations can be rather complex, however, others are readily adapted. For example, consider a company that is educating personnel on telephone communication etiquette and skills. What better way to role play than to use the telephone or audio conferencing!

Course Equipment Requirements

Hands on equipment training will involve more detailed consideration for transitioning a course. Is any special equipment required for learners to complete the course. Can the equipment be made available at the remote sites? What are the safety considerations when working on the equipment? Some equipment can be adapted to a computer-based simulation, which may provide greater instructional flexibility and can decrease the training time required on the actual equipment.

Instructional Support Materials Available

Do some of your courses already have excellent print-based or computer-based instructional materials? These may be some of your most successful distance learning courses. One example that Rick was involved in was a three-week program for administrative clerks. The instructor already had an outstanding learner workbook and job aids that guided students through each of the course tasks. It took less than 60 days for that course to be transitioned. By delivering the course via distance learning the annual cost savings over residential instruction was just under $300,000.

Let's consider an example of selecting a course for distance learning delivery. ABC, Inc. offers dozens of residential and on-site instructor-led courses in the areas of management skills, human resources training, and communication skills. They feel that they will have a competitive advantage if they can deliver some of these courses directly to their customers' workplaces via distance learning. Their distance learning team is preparing the cost-benefit analysis and is selecting potential courses. They currently have a three-day time management seminar that is one of their most popular courses and has a backlog of requests. It is taught through a combination of lecture, written practical exercises and a computer-based in-box prioritization simulation. The learner support materials are very extensive. The distance learning team quickly identifies the course as one that has tremendous potential for return on investment and to position ABC, Inc. as a 21st century training company.

The above factors should act as guidelines. No one factor should cause you to not select a course. We are continually impressed with creative instructional designers and instructors who find ways to deliver courses effectively via distance learning that at first glance others dismissed as non-candidates. With the above guidelines in hand, you can review potential courses and select those that will be included in your team's cost-benefit document.

Identifying Your Current Training Output

This information is the base load of your current training environment. When you look at where you want to go with the distance learning training options, start with your current foundation. Here are the key statistics that you want to identify and quantify based on your on-site or resident training programs for a fiscal year:

- number of courses
- number of class hours
- number of learners
- number of trainers
- average number of learners per class.

Be sure to provide the numbers for all mandated, functional, and soft-skill courses in your organization.

Analyzing Costs Associated With Travel and Lost Productivity

This analysis puts the spotlight on the high cost of traveling to training sites. You will want to list the dollar costs associated with each of the following:

- costs of training travel (including transportation, hotel, food, telephone, and the like)
- seminar and workshop fees
- number of learners traveling to training classes
- employee days lost to travel (you can use an average of four to six hours depending on your circumstances)
- employee (learner) salary lost to travel (you can use a midpoint salary range and compute the hourly worth).

Some organizations also list the costs of the trainers' travel and lost productivity salary. Depending on how many trainers are in your organization, this cost may or may not have a large impact on your training budget. If it does, by all means include it!

Assessing the Alternatives Available to Your Organization

Here's where you paint the picture and identify the costs of what will happen if you act in the following ways:

- do nothing to change your training process
- purchase equipment based on your selection of distance learning technologies
- lease equipment based (if possible) on availability of distance learning methods of delivery.

You want to be able to identify both nonrecurring and recurring costs associated with your selection of distance learning options and associated technologies.

Based on the Distance Learning Master Plan Checklist on page 17, your technical staff or consultants, or both have been part of your distance learning initiatives

Sample Distance Learning Costs

Nonrecurring costs	Recurring costs
Chairs and tables for classroom Multimedia PCs	Maintenance fees for capital equipment Telecommunications costs
Distance learning equipment (Note: Based on the type of equipment you select, this category will break down into the equipment components and support materials you need for the technology.)	Extra phone lines for classroom equipment
Development and conversion costs for pilot course(s) to be taught via distance learning	Distance learning training for trainers, instructional development specialists, site facilitators, technical support staff
Installation of equipment (new).	Course development materials
	Student materials needed for each course
	Marketing and communications expenses to advertise courses
	Mailing and telephone costs for student support materials
	Travel expenses for each course
	Course conversion costs
	Front-end analysis for selecting courses for distance learning
	Program management personnel (handling registrations, assessments, evaluations, scheduling of courses)
	Learner support systems (guidance from instructors, staffed Help Desk, etc.)
	Programming costs from commercial providers
	Other costs based on your specific organizational needs

from the start of your journey. At this juncture, they take more of a role in helping to define the costs of both the purchase and leasing options for distance learning equipment. Your cost-justification process includes the active involvement, guidance, and resources of the technical staff.

For this part of your justification process, you will spend time with your technical staff to discuss the options. They have up-to-date information (or can get it) for the different learning technologies. They usually have established working contacts with leading vendors and suppliers of distance learning equipment and can work with you to get the financial information for the cost-justification process. They know whether or not you can lease or purchase equipment and the related costs.

The nonrecurring and recurring costs are a vital part of your cost-benefit analysis. You must include all identified costs to paint a true picture of the savings, cost-avoidance, and return-on-investment for your distance learning system. The example on page 76 shows some of the costs associated with distance learning. Note that the equipment costs are based on whether you purchase or lease, and the variables can be different based on the needs and requirements of your organization. Your technology experts will have the equipment and communication costs for your system (phone lines and both uplink and downlink satellite costs).

Get your distance learning team mobilized to help get this information! This task would be overwhelming for one person. Sharing the research not only makes the task easier, but it helps stimulate a key desired result—involvement from stakeholders and a shared sense of mission. With that momentum, there will be added strength in your numbers.

Chapter Thirteen

Cost-Benefit Analysis Preparation

Introduction

The cost-benefit analysis is the document that will help sell your program. If you look at it in a similar light as preparing a proposal for a key client, you will find that there are many ways to make it both structurally appealing and targeted to those with the power to say yes or no. The finance people are going to be looking for a document that has been well thought out and carefully justified and that reflects making or saving money (in a big way). You should structure your cost-benefit analysis in a progressive, step-by-step manner. Proper positioning of facts, figures, and benefits to your organization will help pave the way to getting funding for your distance learning system.

You have completed the most time-intensive part of your cost-justification process. Now, we'll put it together to present a cohesive and compelling document that will justify distance learning for you and your organization. It is important to visit your finance department to enlist the aid of a key decision maker to help guide you in preparing your document. You will gain the following benefits:

- The finance department will be involved in helping to create a document that it will review for budgeting justification.
- You will ask and members of the department will advise you about the key elements to include in your document. You want to be sure that all of their priorities are detailed in your analysis.
- You can meet with them for guidance and advice on the structure, content, and format of your work in progress.
- You can enlist their aid in compiling the life-cycle cost-benefit statistical spreadsheet. You provide the numbers that you gathered from all items listed earlier, and they can chart and graph the dollars invested, dollars saved, and the calendar point of starting the return-on-investment (ROI) for the organization. Your graphical picture of ROI coupled with savings may be the most looked at section in your document. Having the finance person on your team is very important.

The main components of your cost-benefit analysis should include the following:

Cover Page

List the key people preparing the document in the training, technical, and financial areas as well as other decision makers responsible for writing the document.

OBJECTIVES

State the purpose of this document, why you are preparing it, and what the benefits are to the organization. You have calculated the costs of delivering both resident training and distance learning for a targeted number of courses that you may want to convert to the distance learning format of your choice. We know from research (both historical and your calculations) that distance learning saves a lot of money. You want to position this proposed financial success on page one of your cost-benefit analysis. You want to get everyone's attention quickly, and this type of statement will do it:

> It is estimated that converting 12 courses to our proposed distance learning format(s) for six years will produce travel savings of approximately $8,236,180. The lost productivity time is estimated at $7,964,350. The total estimated savings is $16,200,530 for this first six-year period.

That type of statement gets attention *fast*. Then, you can move on to list the main areas of your cost-benefit analysis:

BACKGROUND

Include the following information to explain why you want to offer distance learning:

- results of your training needs assessment summary (indicating the need to meet training requirements of your geographically dispersed workforce)
- reasons why you are requesting distance learning funding
- team members assigned to strategically explore distance learning options
- research to validate the efficiencies and cost-effectiveness of the type of equipment you are recommending
- research to validate the effectiveness of distance learning (comparison of resident training assessments vs. learning at a distance)
- site visits to organizations that utilize the type of system you are recommending.

ASSUMPTIONS

Provide information on which you have based your recommendations, including the following:

- the number of courses to be converted to distance learning in the first phase (see your "objectives" statement highlighting the dollars saved and the number of courses that are the target for distance learning conversion)

- training budget reduction facts, such as travel reduction and training courses
- the number of learners anticipated to go through each course each year.

Alternatives

You will use information you gathered in Chapter Twelve and expand on it to compare the current training practices with those you are proposing. You will provide information on the following:

Current practices. Describe the current training requirements and challenges, targeted learner output based on current budgetary constraints, and number of travel days per learner, per course, and per year.

The purchase of distance learning equipment. State what you are recommending and include the costs in an addendum.

The leasing of distance learning equipment. State what you are recommending and include the costs in an addendum.

Implementation

It is at this point that you lay out the specifics of your proposed system. You have certain requests and a targeted number of courses for the first phase or year of its implementation. In the second phase or year, you may need additional equipment and expect to convert an additional number of courses. This is the place to summarize any additional targeted plans that you have.

Recommendations

Here you spell out the type of system you want—whether satellite, computer-based training, or something else—and the number of sites per phase. Refer to the attached cost-benefit analysis spreadsheet that you prepared with the help of your finance team member. A list of proposed sites should be prepared as a separate addendum.

Summary

Here you repeat the exact wording and financial figures that you listed under "Objectives":

> It is estimated that converting 12 courses to our proposed distance learning format(s) for six years will produce travel savings of approximately $8,236,180. The lost productivity time is estimated at $7,964,350. The total estimated savings is $16,200,530 for this first six-year period.

Your carefully designed document, coupled with your team based presentation were make your chances of getting the dollars for your distance learning system excellent. With that in mind, and focusing on the fact that you will receive specific allocated funding for distance learning, you are ready for the final step: implementation and making it all happen for you and your organization.

Implementing Distance Learning

At this point in your distance learning journey, you have gathered a lot of data and information about distance learning technologies and their related costs. You also have visited various sites that are using several different types of delivery options. Based on your training needs assessment and organizational objectives, you prepared a sound cost-benefit analysis and received funding. You're now ready for implementation. This section includes a guide to

- strategic plan development
- program management
- equipment installation
- transitioning residential training courses
- instructional design considerations
- train-the-trainer preparation
- remote site materials preparation and development
- remote site coordination
- course evaluation tool development
- learner support system design.

Chapter Fourteen

Strategic Plan Development

Introduction

Every successful training initiative starts with a sound plan. We have listed elements that both of us have used in establishing a foundation for the implementation of distance learning systems. Your needs might dictate additions, deletions, or adaptations to make the initiative work within your corporate culture and organizational requirements.

This plan will become part of your overall corporate strategic plan and be integrated into your training business plan. You may have extensive experience in preparing both corporate and business unit plans, and the information contained in this section can be tailored to fit your corporate planning guidelines. Of course, every plan should be tied to the mission of your organization. It would be a sound idea to reference any area of your distance learning plan that specifically aligns with your mission statement and corporate strategic objectives.

Strategic Plan Components

Your plan should include several key areas and be written in lay language. Technical jargon should not be included, even though it may seem to some people that you're with-it in knowing the technical playing field. Many people will read your plan, including people with no technical experience. The goal is to have a sound plan to enable you to achieve distance learning success right from the start. To do that, many people in your organization will need to play an important part in decisions relating to funding, design, development, delivery, and maintenance of your system. Therefore, your plan needs to be clear, easy-to-read, and cohesive, and it has to contribute to your organization's bottom line.

Following is an overview of the plan components:

- executive summary
- purpose and requirements
- program management
- training, course development, and support systems
- marketing and communications
- distance learning equipment
- transmission network
- implementation and funding
- appendix: cost-benefit analysis.

As we begin to look at each of these components for your plan, keep in mind the specific needs and requirements for your organization. We'll start with the first page, where distance learning *instant* impressions (and sometimes decision mindsets) are often formed.

Executive Summary

The executive summary provides a two- to three-page overview of your distance learning strategic plan document. Remember that this summary may be the only part of the plan that a decision maker reads at a first examination. It must immediately capture the reader's attention.

The executive summary is a global look at your major workforce challenges, multilevel workforce, changing needs and priorities, and competitive threats and opportunities, and it should show how distance learning can help with these issues.

Begin your executive summary with a paragraph or two that answers the questions, "Why are we implementing distance learning?" and "How will the program contribute to our organization's role and mission?" In the next paragraph, answer the question, "How will distance learning be integrated with existing training initiatives and goals?" or "How will it complement them?" Analyze in your own mind how other projects and training programs will be enhanced by the integration of distance learning methods of delivery. Explain in a few sentences the strong link between distance learning and these important (and probably already funded) projects. Aligning bottom-line benefits with corporate goals and competitive directions on the first page of your document would be a good strategy.

Purpose and Requirements

Every organizational initiative should be profitable and tied to goal achievement. Distance learning must support the achievement of selected training initiatives and organizational goals. All efforts and results must be targeted to helping increase profitability and must be explained in this part of your plan.

You want to identify the role of your organization by stating your current mission. Once again, the parallel process of aligning mission with recommended distance learning training delivery methods can help to ensure that you are going in the right direction. Any recommendations should show this relationship.

Under "Purpose and Requirements," you should answer these questions:

- Why were distance learning methods of delivery explored?
- What environmental elements caused the training department to look at different methods of training delivery?
- How did the workforce needs assessment drive the exploration of using distance learning technologies? (Identification of the skills—both functional and nonfunctional—needed by every level in the workforce).
- What type and level of performance output is needed to remain competitive?
- In what way did the travel or training budget allocations have an impact on finding more cost-effective solutions to delivering training?
- What bottom-line changes will occur with training via distance learning?

- What will more cost-effective and just-in-time training mean as a competitive advantage?

Most organizations are going through change. The adage "The only thing constant is change" applies. You can help position the need for distance learning whatever challenges you are facing, including the following:

- competition
- global customer base (internal and or external, or both)
- reduction in travel and training budgets
- retraining requirements for new skills
- new technologies in the workplace (both internal and external customers)
- reengineering training delivery for immediate workforce access.

The "Purpose and Requirements" part of your plan should explain why the organization needs to change and how this change can occur by using distance learning. The plan for change should include the requirements for change. What needs to be different? Provide a clear explanation of why you are implementing a distance learning program and form the transition into the next part of the plan, which describes how to make it happen.

Program Management

The "Program Management" part of the plan describes the roles, responsibilities, and importance of key people who will manage the distance learning program and system. This part of the plan should help to clearly identify those individuals who will play a vital role and be the core members of the distance learning team. It also should provide a model for identifying who does what by clearly defining responsibilities and creating a synergistic environment free of ambiguity. It is critical to the success of the distance learning initiative. Chapter Fifteen provides an expanded look at the elements of effective distance learning program management.

Training, Course Development, and Support Systems

In this section, describe the training that must be provided to trainers, instructional designers, remote site coordinators, and administrators of the distance learning system. Tell what needs to be done and how it will be accomplished. Also describe the process that your organization uses to identify, prioritize, and develop distance learning courses and events. These descriptions should include the appropriate staff and learner support systems. Chapters Seventeen through Twenty-Three address in depth the components of training, course development, and support systems. These chapters present "how-to-do-it" aspects that can be adapted easily to meet your organization's unique requirements.

Marketing and Communications

This section of the plan describes how you plan to market the distance learning initiative within your organization. Implementing distance learning is a major change. Effective marketing of the initiative and continuous communications can help to prevent misunderstandings and prepare the organization for this new approach to training delivery. As well, your marketing initiatives will be a vital link to communicating features, advantages, and benefits to your target audience. It is often difficult for many people to embrace this new way of learning unless they clearly see, and have constant reinforcement of, how they will benefit. Therefore, it is very important to include an outline of your marketing strategy in the plan.

The marketing strategy you use should communicate the objectives of the initiative, general information about how distance learning will affect the organization, and specific information about upcoming distance events or courses to personnel throughout the organization. Remember the team approach, and identify others within your organization who can assist you in this communication effort.

Your organization may already have several corporate communication tools in place. These might include

- e-mail
- fax
- company memorandums
- brochures
- videotapes
- town hall meetings
- an intranet.

All of the above are potential vehicles you may use to "get the word out." Describe which tools are to be used and how they are to be used to disseminate information on the initiative in this section of the plan.

Many organizations develop a unique logo for their distance learning initiative. The logo is then used on all communication that is distributed regarding the initiative. This adds a professional touch and helps those throughout the organizations quickly identify distance learning information. The logo also can be used on remote site materials that are provided to learners. (See Chapter Twenty.) If you choose to develop a logo, introduce it in this section of the plan. Explain how the logo was developed and any special significance it has.

Your target training audience will probably become very excited as they understand how distance learning can increase their education and training opportunities. So trainees need accurate information about the initiative and what they need to do to participate. Be sure to include how you will market specific events and courses to the learners in this section. The learners are the focus of the training delivered via distance learning. The learners also should be the focus of your marketing and communication strategy.

Distance Learning Equipment

This capital investment portion of the plan describes the equipment that your organization needs to use at both the origination (trainer) and remote (learner) sites. This part of your plan should not be one of specifications and techno-babble, rather it should help readers gain a basic understanding of what is going to be installed at the various sites. In addition, it should explain how the equipment will be integrated with any telecommunications or multimedia training systems already in place. Chapter Sixteen outlines the steps to consider in developing an installation plan for distance learning equipment.

Transmission Network

In this part of the strategic plan, outline the existing and planned telecommunications and information management infrastructures of your distance learning program. Here your technical team members should help describe and detail the technical components of both the equipment and transmission network information. They should prepare the information according to the training requirements that you provide. They also should look at the anticipated number of courses and desired method of delivery and analyze which transmission medium is most cost-effective.

This section explains the impact that distance learning will have on any existing systems. It also lists new networks or systems that will be required to support each phase of your distance learning system. Transmission networks for distance learning provide the path that the electronic signal takes from a trainer's site to the learners', or remote, site. The options for transmission medium include electrons traveling through the air (by satellite or microwave) or electrons traveling over cables and wires in the ground (by phone lines, fiber-optic cables, or coaxial cables like those from your local cable-TV company).

Each of these transmission medium have advantages and disadvantages depending on the application. Satellite is often used when there are a large number of sites. Phone lines and fiber optics are most commonly used when the number of sites is relatively small and the distances are confined to a specific region. In many cases, the distance learning transmission medium is not one or the other but a combination, or hybrid, of satellite, phone lines, and fiber-optic cable.

Your organization already has an existing transmission infrastructure in place for its telecommunications needs. When placing a phone call or transferring information via computer, you are using that transmission medium. It may be possible to use that infrastructure for your distance learning needs. More likely than not, your organization will need to modify or expand the infrastructure to accommodate the distance learning requirements.

Remember to keep this section of your plan in an overview format. This is not the place for pages and pages of wiring diagrams. It is the place to explain, using a broad brush, how the trainer's electrons will travel to the learner sites and what the relationship of this transmission is to existing corporate infrastructures.

Implementation and Funding Plan

As excited as you are by the prospect of implementing distance learning, you surely realize one important point—it is not going to happen all at once. Remember the ancient wisdom, "Rome did not implement distance learning in a day!"

Use this section to describe and graph the implementation timelines, milestones, and funding cycles for your distance learning program. Include the phases of the implementation, the activities during each phase, and the resources needed to make the program happen.

You are probably already familiar with good project management techniques. Your organization may have standardized processes for outlining the various phases of any major project. Project management software also is available to help produce the required reports, charts, and timelines.

Clearly, certain events must happen before others. For example, you will probably not purchase much equipment before you receive funding. However, some events can take place at the same time you are working to accomplish other tasks. Begin to benchmark and conduct pilot events while you are working on your cost-benefit analysis. The size of your distance learning team, the amount of time the members are able to dedicate to distance learning, and the degree of teamwork will largely determine the implementation timelines.

Your finance team member can help to write and illustrate the part of this section that explains what funding will be available during the various phases. This information cannot be overlooked. Some plans have come to a grinding halt because the available resources needed for implementation have not been considered or reported adequately.

Cost-Benefit Analysis

Include a cost-benefit analysis as an appendix to your strategic plan. It provides the readers with an understanding of the level of effort undertaken to ensure that the distance learning initiative contributes to the organization's profitability or effectiveness and does not detract from it.

In this chapter we have outlined the key elements that your distance learning team should include in your organization's strategic plan. The plan is a team effort requiring consensus and joint ownership. By addressing these elements as a team and creating a written plan, you can develop and present a document that is the map for your distance learning journey.

You will need support for your distance learning effort from key decision makers in your organization. It is likely that they will ask, "Where is the plan?" If you have followed the steps in this chapter, adapted them to address your organization's particular needs, and created a strategic planning document, then you can look forward to that question. It will give you an opportunity to share your team's collective planning vision.

If you have a great plan but fail to take any action on it, then you are not much better off than an organization without any plan. In the remaining chapters in this section, we address the critical action steps that must take place so that your team can be successful in implementing and institutionalizing distance learning within your organization.

CHAPTER FIFTEEN

Program Management

INTRODUCTION

What factor contributes more to the success of your distance learning initiative than any other? What factor, if overlooked, could create constant obstacles, challenges, delays, and roadblocks? What factor, if correctly applied, could help to overcome unforeseen problems and multiply your effectiveness several times over? The factor is the organization and functioning of a cohesive distance learning team that effectively contributes to and manages the design, development, implementation, and maintenance of your program.

You will not be able to go it alone as a trainer, nor should you want to. Distance learning requires establishing collaborative working relationships that previously may not have been required. To reach your goals and accomplish your objectives, you need a true team approach, not a turf approach.

In this chapter we provide a step-by-step approach that you can use to successfully establish a distance learning implementation team. We also help to identify what steps are necessary for this team to begin to act as the body that provides guidance, oversight, and action to managing your organization's distance learning initiative. Effective program management involves these five key steps:

- Identify key individuals as distance learning team members.
- Establish the team structure.
- Assess the team's awareness and understanding of issues and needs.
- Define the roles, functions, and responsibilities of team members.
- Set a team goal for publication of the draft of the distance learning strategic plan and begin work together on the plan.

Now let's look more closely at each of these steps. The implementation of each step varies somewhat from organization to organization, but the basic steps remain the same. As you review each step, think of how the step can be implemented most effectively within your specific corporate culture and environment.

IDENTIFY KEY INDIVIDUALS AS DISTANCE LEARNING TEAM MEMBERS

The nature of distance learning, with its technology and telecommunications, requires the involvement of and contributions from different functional experts. However, there are many more relationships involved, which are less obvious but no less important.

Consider the funding of your distance learning effort. It requires some new budgeting approaches that are not as clearly defined or clear-cut as in the past. For example, when using a telecommunications system for training, should the dollars be funded to the telecommunications division or the training division? Should a separate telecommunications system be funded to support the distance learning program? Who determines what priority the funding for training delivery receives compared to other demands on the telecommunications dollars? Regardless of the answers, you can see that your comptroller or chief financial officer needs to be involved in ways that previously may not have been required.

The list of new functions and cross-functional relationships goes on. Take a moment to pull out an extra copy of your organizational chart. Using a highlighter, mark the key decision makers that you think could possibly play an important role in the successful implementation of your distance learning program. Now with another highlighter, identify the program managers within the organization who work for the key decision makers and who the decision makers will probably assign to the distance learning project. These personnel will form the nucleus of your distance learning project action team, advisory group, committee, work group, or whatever terminology is appropriate for your organization.

This would be an appropriate time to consider whether an outside consultant or distance learning specialist should be a part of your distance learning team. A consultant can assist in the design, development, implementation, and maintenance of your program. There are many benefits to having help from an experienced guide with an objective view that is external to the organization. The consultant can provide insights based on distance learning efforts of organizations similar to yours. A consultant or specialist can save hundreds of hours that you would otherwise have to spend researching alternatives and learning from your own pioneering experience.

Evaluate External Resources

Some key areas to consider when evaluating potential contractors or consultants include the following:

Client references. The best indicator of how a consultant might do working with you is to check referrals and discuss the qualities, expertise, and end results that the consultant provided for those clients. Ask for a referral list with all contact information.

Distance learning certification from an accredited university. This can help ensure that a consultant is well versed in all aspects of both the technical and human side of distance learning. Additionally, professional certification brings experience and expertise in knowing how to effectively manage a distance learning system.

Experience and background in design and delivery of training and education. Understanding the needs of adult learners is vital to help guide the learner-centered initiatives for each aspect of your distance learning system.

A list of the distance learning technologies that the consultant has experience with. Some consultants are experts in one of the distance learning media but have little experience or exposure to other media. Choosing a contractor who has a limited vision will result in a fairly narrow application of technologies. The consultant's pet medium may become the only recommended solution. Pick a specialist who has experience with a variety of distance learning delivery options or whose team includes specialists in different methods.

Once you have decided on whether to include an outside specialist or not, you have completed the first step in program management—identifying the key individuals who should be part of your distance learning team.

Establish the Team Structure

You should decide whether it is appropriate to designate a chairperson or leader for the group and how decisions should be made. The structure should be consistent with your organizational processes. Whether decisions are made by unanimous consensus, by a team majority, or at the chairperson's discretion is dependent on your organizational processes and culture. The team will have some important decisions to make, and it will be helpful to have the decision-making process established at the very beginning.

Early in the process is also a good time to determine a schedule of team meetings that will keep everyone involved and informed on a continuous basis. It is important to keep meetings scheduled every month or two at the same designated time. This timetable allows team members to plan and structure any other meetings accordingly. It is important to stress the critical nature of each team member's attendance at each meeting.

Assess Team Awareness and Understanding of Issues and Needs

With your team in place, assess the members' perceptions of distance learning and their level of understanding. As part of this process, provide them with an overview of distance learning. This can usually be done in a four-hour session. Take a moment right now to thumb through sections one, two, and five of this book. These sections can serve as an outline of what to cover with the team, although you need not go into the same depth we did. If you are using an outside consultant, you can assign that person the task of presenting this initial workshop for your staff. This is often a good idea for the introduction because the consultant is well versed in handling the many frequently asked questions about distance learning.

Define the Roles, Functions, and Responsibilities of Team Members

The fourth step should be done as a team with everyone providing input. The job aid on page 95 will help serve as a guide to what will be done and which team member or members will take and be accountable for assigned responsibilities.

You may choose to outsource some of the responsibilities or tasks. The decision to outsource will depend on your current level of staffing, other projects, and the degree of organizational flexibility in assigning personnel to cross-functional projects. If you choose to outsource, it is important to carefully evaluate potential vendors or contractors to ensure that they have the proven ability to perform the tasks that you require and a proven track record of distance learning related projects.

Set a Team Goal

With steps one through four completed, you are ready to move significantly forward as a team on your distance learning journey. In addition to the long-term goal identified in your distance learning mission statement, the team should set a goal for publishing the distance learning strategic plan discussed in Chapter Fourteen. Completing the foregoing steps also provides the information you need for part one of the strategic plan.

Team Responsibilities Checklist

WHAT? Function or Task	WHO? Division Responsible	WHEN? Target Date
Overall Administration of Distance Learning Initiative		
Overall program administration		
Development of budget for distance learning implementation and ongoing initiative		
Acquisition of funding to support distance learning budget		
Marketing courses and events to appropriate training audience		
Registration of students for the event or course		
Curricula Development, Instructor Training, and Course Delivery		
Training of curricula development personnel in design of courses that will be taught at a distance		
Development or adaption of curricula and courses to be taught at a distance		
Training of instructors and trainers in teaching at a distance		
Training courses and events via distance learning		
Evaluation of distance learning events and courses		
Selection of distance learning equipment based on training needs		
Selection/ Installation of Distance Learning Equipment and Infrastructure		
Selection of distance learning transmission medium or media based on training needs		
Installation of distance learning transmission medium or media		
Installation of distance learning equipment		
Training of personnel on distance learning equipment		
Remote Site Coordination and Administration		
Selection and training of remote site facilitators		
Scheduling the use of the remote sites for various courses events		
Preparation of equipment and classroom at the remote site for a course or events		
Remote site facilitation of the actual course or event		

Chapter Sixteen

Equipment Installation

Introduction

This chapter is not meant for you as a trainer alone. It takes a team effort with your technical support personnel to accomplish the objectives outlined in this chapter. You will provide valuable insights into the training requirements that will help the technical folks to best meet the needs of the learners.

After reading Section Two, you have a good overview of the various distance learning technologies and the equipment involved in delivering training using different media. During implementation, the equipment is installed at various locations to support the delivery of training. You probably have some of the following questions at this point:

- How do I plan for this installation?
- Which sites do I schedule for installation first?
- What preparation should be done?
- If I'm using a suite of distance learning tools, do I put them all in at once?
- What if I receive only a portion of the funding expected for equipment?
- Should personnel receive special training on the use of the equipment?

This chapter will help you to answer those questions. At the conclusion, your team should be able to begin to develop an equipment installation plan. The key steps in developing an equipment installation plan are as follows:

- Identify the locations of learners and instructors.
- Plot the remote and origination sites on a map.
- Determine the equipment needs for each remote and origination site.
- Develop a site preparation plan.
- Develop an installation timeline for equipment delivery
- Develop a training plan for equipment usage.
- Prepare the sites for the equipment.
- Deliver and install the equipment.
- Train personnel on the equipment.
- Monitor usage, maintenance, and personnel support.

Identify the Locations of Learners and Instructors

You can restate this step another way: Identify possible remote sites and origination sites. Identifying the locations helps the trainer and technical support personnel to focus on where the functional requirements are for your training program.

To determine where your remote distance learning sites should be, ask yourself these questions:

- Where is our training audience located?
- Are there a number of existing regional locations or offices?
- Can some of the offices share a distance learning classroom, or should each office have its own capability?
- Do the existing locations have a classroom for training?
- Is there any staffing currently at the existing locations for training support or audiovisual support?

To help identify your origination sites or instructor sites, ask yourself:

- What are the locations of the instructors that provide the training?
- Where do employees currently travel to attend training?

Now create the two lists: one of the locations of the training audience and the other of the instructors. If someone on your team can enter the lists into a database program, you will be a step ahead. By having the information in a database, you can later use it to track the installation schedules, teaching schedules, and various aspects associated with managing the status of your site locations. A database program can also interface with mapping software described in the next step.

Plot the Remote and Origination Sites on a Map

Once you have created your lists of instructor and learner sites, you can plot the locations of remote and origination sites on a map to see how many distance learning sites will be required to support your training objectives. A number of commercially available software packages can assist you in mapping the locations. These packages use the zip codes from your database or site list to automatically plot the location on a map.

The mapping software also allows you to view the locations in relation to existing regional boundaries. Additionally, it provides you with a way to query the information to determine distances between facilities. For example, you may have a major regional office that has several district offices within 60 miles. Appendix A lists some of the currently available mapping software packages.

Determine the Equipment Needs for Each Remote and Origination Site

You have several options when considering what equipment to install to implement a successful distance learning program. Following are four basic alternatives:

Purchase and install a complete suite of distance learning equipment at each of your remote sites and instructor sites. This immediately allows you to do audio teletraining, audiographic conferencing, interactive television, video teleconferencing, computer-based training, and online computer training at all possible locations.

Install some of the distance learning equipment described in section two at each of your remote sites and instructor sites. This would allow you to begin training at all sites with a subset of the tools. For example, you could start with audio teletraining and audiographic conferencing. Later, you could expand the equipment to include other capabilities such as video teleconferencing or interactive television.

Install a complete suite of distance learning equipment at some of your remote sites and instructor sites. This would allow you to begin training with all of the capabilities within a region or specific group of sites. You can later add the additional sites to complete installation at all of your remote sites and instructor sites.

Install some of the distance learning equipment at some of your remote sites and instructor sites. For example, you might choose a specific region and install the equipment that would allow training with video teleconferencing. Later you could install additional equipment and additional sites to complete installation of all sites with all equipment.

Several factors will influence which alternative you choose. The most obvious is your budget and resources available for purchasing and installing the equipment. Additionally, you may want to begin with a regional approach because of a unique training requirement specific to that area. Weigh the alternatives based on the resources you have. Get those on your team involved in the process as the final choice will affect them as well.

Develop a Site Preparation Plan

Depending on the equipment chosen, various degrees of site preparation will be necessary to accommodate the equipment. In some cases, all you will need is to ensure that a standard telephone line is installed in the room where the equipment will be set up. In other cases, for example video teleconferencing, more extensive preparation will be needed. This preparation might include installing special high bandwidth telephone lines or fiber-optic cable; room painting to acquire the contrast necessary for video teleconferencing; special lighting placement; and camera mounting preparation. Before you panic, stop. Catch your breath! This is a team effort. The chances are that the technical folks on your distance learning team are familiar with these types of requirements.

The degree of preparation will also vary with the condition of each of your sites. Some buildings may have concrete walls, floors, and ceilings. Other buildings may have drop tile ceilings and raised floors built for running telecommunications cables. Obviously, the degree of preparation needed for each site would be very different.

To determine the appropriate degree of preparation and any unusual requirements, your technical team members should have a site survey done. Most sites will fit the category of "no unusual preparation needed." However, it is much better to discover any exceptions before the equipment is delivered and you find that it cannot be installed.

One of the more interesting challenges discovered in a site survey was at distance learning remote site that the United States Air National Guard had selected in Alaska. Due largely to excellent management of the equipment installation process and thorough site surveys, the Guard discovered early on that it had a significant challenge—a mountain range. The Air National Guard distance learning system uses satellite delivery. No matter what options the team looked at for mounting the satellite dish at the remote location, the line of sight required for the dish to receive the satellite signal was obstructed by a mountain range. We hope you will not have to move mountains at your remote sites. If you do, at least you will find out during a site survey!

Develop an Installation Timeline for Equipment Delivery

Preparing sites, installing equipment, and training people to use the equipment all take time and should be well coordinated. As soon as people at the remote sites find out about the distance learning project and the equipment that is going to be installed, they will ask your team, "When are we going to get it?" (It may remind you of the usual family car trip question, "Are we there yet?"). A well-prepared timeline that shows the site survey, site preparation, installation, and training dates should be distributed to help them see the big picture and where they fit in.

Develop a Training Plan for Equipment Usage

Before putting your equipment in place, you will want to develop a training plan for the people who will be expected to operate it. Once the equipment has been delivered, the folks at the remote sites will be anxious to use it. It is important to invest time at the onset to ensure that they become confident in using it; the trial-and-error method of instruction will not instill that confidence. Many organizations use distance learning to accomplish this training. Ford Motor Company broadcasts weekly sessions to new FordStar distance learning network sites to help ensure that the equipment is operational. These sessions also provide training opportunities in case there has been personnel turnover at the remote sites.

Topics to cover during equipment training include the following:

- How do I turn it on?
- Do I turn it off? How?
- Whom do I contact if it doesn't work?
- Is there a troubleshooting checklist I should follow before I call for help?
- How do I store the equipment?
- How do I use it to participate in a training event?
- Are there any special environmental considerations (room temperature, humidity, leaky roofs)?

Benchmark with other organizations. How do they train personnel on the use of the equipment? What lessons have they learned?

Some vendors may have promised you that the equipment is so user friendly that little or no training will be needed. We have discovered that it is far better to plan for more equipment training than is needed than to underplan. You want to ensure that your training events will not be interrupted by technical problems that additional training could have prevented. Remember, "An ounce of equipment training is worth a pound of technical troubleshooting."

Prepare the Sites for the Equipment

Your site survey determined the specific preparation that was needed. Obviously you will need to draw up a timeline for that preparation before the equipment arrives. Give yourself some extra time because Murphy's Law—Anything that can go wrong will— may strike. You will want this step to be carefully done so that the equipment installation in the next step will go smoothly.

Deliver and Install The Equipment

It is likely that an equipment vendor and your technical support personnel will be accomplishing this step. The important point is to have an operational checklist that must be completed prior to signing off on the installation. You want your classrooms to be ready for users at the completion of installation. You don't want problems that require return visits from the vendor.

Train personnel on the Equipment

You already have a training plan. Now it is time to put it into action. Be sure to evaluate the training (see Chapter Twenty-Two) so that you can constantly improve. Often, we cannot anticipate all the questions that users may ask. The personnel who will operate the equipment can provide you with advice on how to improve the training for those personnel who will be trained in the future.

Monitor Usage, Maintenance, and Personnel Support

By this step, you should have a database of your site locations. You can use this database to monitor the usage at the sites. You should also record any maintenance that is needed and the personnel support required to operate the site. This information can help you to quickly identify problem equipment, support personnel training needs, and sites that may soon require additional capabilities.

By following these steps as a team, you will soon have a network of reliable distance learning sites run by well-trained support personnel. You are now ready to offer courses over that network. As the technical people were planning the installation of the equipment, you as a trainer have been busy working with the instructional designers and instructors. The next chapter explains the steps that are required so that as the equipment is installed, the employees can begin benefiting from courses that are taught via distance learning.

Chapter Seventeen

Transitioning Residential Training Courses

Introduction

You and your team are ready to go through the process in which some courses that are taught in residence are offered via distance learning. This process is known as "transitioning." How do you transition a course? There are the following eight basic steps in this process:

- Review the course's present state.
- Determine appropriate technologies to deliver the training.
- Prepare a life-cycle cost estimate for the course and choose the media.
- Decide whether to transition the course internally or through outsourcing.
- Transition the course.
- Deliver the course or training.
- Evaluate the effectiveness.
- Adjust and transition as necessary.

Review the Course's Present State

Before you begin to transition a course, it is helpful for you to get a good sense of the present state of that course. You should do this review as a team that includes the trainers or instructors, course developers, appropriate members of your distance learning team, and if possible, employees who have recently completed the course. Each course or training event usually has a lesson plan of some sort that the trainer or instructor uses as a guide in teaching the course. Additionally, there are visual aids that accompany the course. These materials should be readily available to all team members during the review. Some of the key questions to consider during the review include

- What is the objective of the course or training?

- How long is the course? If you subtract administrative time (meals, breaks, etc.), how long is the course?

- Is the course broken down into submodules? How many? What are the major topic areas?

- How many times is the course taught each year?

- What is the cost of conducting each iteration of the course?
- Who is the intended audience?
- What percentage of the entire target audience is trained each year?
- If the number of employees trained each year is significantly different from the number of employees who should receive the training, what are the constraining factors?
- How do you currently evaluate learners' achievement of the course objectives? Are there written exams, tests, or practical exercises that are graded?
- What happens to learners who fail a particular exercise or test?
- Who certifies that a learner has successfully completed the course? How is the employee's record annotated to show credit for completing the course?

At the conclusion of this review, all members of the team should have a common understanding of the present state of the course.

Determine Appropriate Technologies to Deliver the Training

Refer to the media selection matrix in Section Two. As you recall, this matrix helps you to choose the appropriate media based on the task that you are training. You have probably noticed that for some tasks, multiple media might be appropriate. Further refinement is now necessary. You will need to select one medium or make a conscious decision that you will be offering various media to train the same task.

Why would a trainer choose more than one medium to train the same task? Let's consider an example. ABC Corporation has a company policy that requires all employees to receive annual training on hazardous materials handling. The instructors use several live video motion clips to emphasize the proper procedures when dealing with certain hazardous materials. In using the matrix, the team decides that either interactive television or computer-based training would be equally appropriate. Team members prefer interactive television because they want to have live interaction with the employees. However, they also would like the same material available to employees in a high-quality interactive CD-ROM. They envision offering the course live once each quarter and requiring that all employees attend a session to meet the mandated training requirement. They also would like the CD-ROM to be available so that employees can use it on demand for refresher training between the live offerings. They also see the CD-ROM as a tool for new employees to use who are hired between sessions.

Also consider that a training team may use multiple media during different portions of a course. For example, the first module might be most appropriately taught using video teleconferencing, but the second module would be better suited to interactive television. Multiple media would not be very practical for courses or events that are only a day or two in duration. However, for courses that are several weeks long, mixing the media can help reduce costs and increase learner participation, and it can enable trainers to match technology to lessons in the course.

The team is now ready to analyze how budget dollars may affect their decision in the choice of media. This is part of step 3.

Prepare Life-Cycle Cost Estimate for Course and Choose the Media

As part of the review process, a number of variables were considered to help with this step. With the assistance of your technical team, you should be able to figure what the annual costs will be for a course or event depending on the medium that you choose. It would also be helpful to review section four, including some of the examples on analyzing the costs associated with delivery of the course. These costs may drive your media decision.

The costs associated with optimizing a course for various media can vary greatly. The development of computer-based training can range from $5,000 to $15,000 per course hour. The costs of producing scripts and optimizing graphics for delivery via interactive television or video teleconferencing depend greatly on the complexity of the tasks or course being taught. Development for delivery via the Internet or intranet is still fairly new and standardized costs are not yet available.

Along with the development costs, it is important to consider the training delivery costs. Video teleconferencing and interactive television development costs are usually pretty close for a given course or event. However, the delivery costs for these two media will vary greatly depending on the number of remote sites and carrier transmission costs.

Let's revisit the previous example of ABC Corporation and the course in hazardous materials handling. Even though the team would also like to develop a CD-ROM, members estimate that the costs to develop it are not within their current year training budget. They shelve that idea and will revisit it as they put together next year's training budget. They decide that initially they will deliver the course once each quarter via interactive television. They also decide to videotape the live instruction and make those tapes available to employees as an alternative way of meeting the refresher training requirement until they can budget for the CD-ROM development.

Transition the Course Internally or Through Outsourcing

Regardless of what kind of media you have chosen, you now have to make a decision. Will you transition the course using internal resources, and staff or will you contract it out? The answer will depend on your organization's current resources and the staff's experience.

Some of the organizations we have worked with have existing television production capabilities. Most were using the facilities for producing videotapes, not for live interactive instruction. However, many of the principles and skills associated with producing a quality videotape also apply to producing a quality interactive television or video teleconferencing course. If the workload can be managed, with some additional training, the video production personnel can become an in-house asset for the production of distance learning courses and events.

If your organization lacks the necessary internal staffing or resources, you will have to outsource the development. **To test the capabilities of the contractor or**

organization you are considering working with, choose a short course or event before you commit to a large project. Nothing is as reliable as proven observable performance. By choosing one of your shorter courses or a daylong training event, you will be able to see if your prospective contractor can deliver on time and within budget. Visit organizations that are already outsourcing and get referrals from them.

Transition the Course

This step is where the actual work is done. It is a matter of your team's taking the existing course materials, visual aids, and the like, and asking yourselves, "How will we do this effectively with the media we have chosen?" Of course, if you have outsourced this task, the contractor should be asking those questions.

There are some excellent references and resources available on the design of graphics for video presentation. Refer to Appendix C for some suggested references. Again, visit with organizations already doing training at a distance. How did they modify their courses? Also the interactive strategies are extremely important. How can you build in interaction with the learners? The cardinal rule is, interact early and often! Make it purposeful and directly related to the objectives.

Whether you develop the course internally or outsource the work, use your best project management skills during this step. Have clearly assigned milestones and costs associated with the various steps. Hold yourselves or the contractor to those milestones. Try to capture as many lessons learned from the process as possible so that the next course becomes easier.

Deliver the Course or Training

Of course all the preparation and related steps are designed to meet a training need and to deliver the training to employees. Remember that this is a training session and not a network television show.

Rick Gividen remembers watching one manager as she observed her organization's first distance learning event, which was delivered via interactive television. The manager had a copy of the script and was agitated when the camera angle did not change on cue or when the graphics were delayed even a few seconds. She was making a common mistake. She knew the script and when everything was supposed to happen to the second. She needed to be reminded to look at the event from the learners' perspectives. The event turned out to be tremendously successful for them. Thousands of employees were trained. The employees never noticed that the camera shot wasn't changed or that the graphics were two or three sentences behind in a couple of instances.

Of course you will want to videotape the event or record it on audiotape if audiographics or audio teletraining were used. This will provide a helpful record for later review.

Evaluate the Effectiveness

If possible, use the same tests, practical exercises, or exams that are administered in the residential course. They will provide an easy way to demonstrate the effectiveness of distance learning. There are already reams and reams of research on the effectiveness of distance learning, and it shows that it works! However, it is always nice to be able to use an in-house comparison to help win over those who may be somewhat hesitant (or downright hostile!).

You will also want to develop a brief questionnaire to measure learners' reactions to being taught at a distance. Be advised that learners may not necessarily prefer what helps them to learn best. There are a number of cases where distance learning learners said they would have preferred residential instruction, but their performance on course exams exceeded that of their residential counterparts. (See Chapter Twenty-Two.)

Adjust and Transition as Necessary

The delivery of courses and events is a continuous improvement process. Based on your evaluations, you should have some information that can help you to do an even better job the next time around.

Carefully review the videotapes or audiotapes, review the written evaluations, and interview some of the employees that received the training. If it can be improved, make the adjustment prior to the next iteration of the course.

By following these steps, you should have walked through the process with one course or event. This can then serve as a model for other courses and events. You may want to modify the eight steps to suit your organization. You are now on your way to having an institutionalized process for taking your residential courses and offering them at a distance.

Chapter Eighteen

Instructional Design Considerations

Introduction

The beginning of the redesign of your existing courses or the development of new courses to be delivered via distance learning is the first major step in the success of your training initiatives.

Before we get into the elements of design, it is important to look at who will be designing your courses. You want to ensure that if you use internal resources, the instructional designers have

- been part of your distance learning team initiatives
- experienced distance learning events, especially with the technologies you have selected
- acquired an awareness and understanding of the distance learning research that's been done on course development (see Appendix C)
- shown a willingness to experiment with creative ways to stimulate learner interactions before, during, and after course delivery.

Distance learning success will be measured at the remote sites. It won't be measured by how jazzy a course looks or the fact that you're using technology to reach the learners. The learners will decide how successful your efforts are by their enthusiasm about how the course is delivered as well as by the application of the content to their own situations. They will judge its effectiveness by both a content assessment evaluation and by how much they enjoyed your method of delivery. Everything in distance learning design and delivery must start with the learner as the center of the training universe.

Selection of Instructional Designers

There are qualities we look for in selecting instructional designers to work on distance learning projects. These important qualities include

- flexibility
- adaptability
- enthusiasm about distance learning opportunities (Not everyone will have it!)
- a learner-centered mindset or a willingness to develop one

- ability to create a creative modularized approach to course content
- ability to design active participation exercises to help involve remote site learners
- knowledge and ability to use multimedia applications to enhance the variety, effectiveness, and enjoyment of the learning experience
- ability to create pre- and post-course learning materials that will strengthen the lessons learned during the live distance learning event
- willingness to move away from the lecture-based training approach
- willingness to work in a team approach to creating course materials.

A tall order? Yes, but each one is very important. Your instructional designers must work in a collaborative fashion with the trainers, multimedia, and distance learning technology experts. All of the items in the list play a vital part in the success of your programs.

Many instructional designers feel comfortable using the instructional systems design (ISD) model as the design for converting courses to distance learning. It's a model that they are familiar with and one that allows a process-oriented approach to use for the design, development, delivery, and ongoing evaluation of your distance learning courses and supporting materials.

The first critical component of instructional design is that learners are in the center of all initiatives—everything starts, continues, and ends with their needs and success. The next component is the structure, content, and length of the course itself.

Distance learning events should be between one and four hours in length. You will lose the learners if you have sessions longer than four hours. How many of us would sit still for a five-hour movie, even if we did get to interact? We would most likely get tired and restless, and our minds would wander to many things other than the movie. Or, we would go to sleep.

To keep the learners awake and engaged in the learning process, you want to structure your learning objectives and content into modular formats with a variety of interaction activities and use of multimedia tools, when and where appropriate.

You may have a course that has eight key learning areas. Break them up into modules that could effectively be taught during the distance learning event. You may want to develop a series approach to a course. You could have, for example, four two-hour course segments. Also prepare your learning support materials or reference guides to be self-contained learning tools. This type of structure will enable your learners to benefit from the live event and to have the opportunity to use the self-directed resource materials at home or on the job.

Learner-centered interaction activities will play a vital role in the success of your course. You can look at the current activities you use now to deliver the course on site, and adapt them for the technology you will be using. You can add new and fun activities to enhance the learning experience. Look at a variety of interaction opportunities to keep your learners engaged in the learning process. Just remember: Build in some type of interaction every five to seven minutes.

When looking at the way Unisys designed its courses for desktop application training, notice that the company used a variety of interactive strategies. Plus, the designers included fun (a very important ingredient, especially for distance learning). Unisys's training incorporated word scrambles, pop quizzes, questions and comments about particular points, and pre-broadcast homework assignments with learners focusing answers on previous learning content.

Use your imagination and create activities that are suited to the technologies you select. Television is a visual medium, and you can design activities where learners can see something before they respond. Or if you are using audio teleconferencing, pre-course readings and work assignments can form the basis of a lively discussion. Look at the technologies you will be using to help determine the type and length of activity.

Be sure to use a media selection guide found on page 52 to help you select multimedia tools that will be effective based on both your learning objectives and the type of technology that will be used for delivering your training. If you currently do not have this guide, there are many resources available to help you select appropriate tools based on your desired learning outcomes and target audience.

Instructional Design Model

The model for instructional design specifically targeted for distance learning was developed by Michael Moore of Pennsylvania State University. He presents the following four levels of learner interaction necessary for effective distance learning:

Learner to Interface

The interface is any method used to convey the learning to the learner: the telephone for audio teleconferencing, the TV monitor for satellite or video teleconferencing, the PC for computer-based training, and print materials for either a live event or self-study modules.

Learner to Content

In distance learning design, instructional designers want to be aware of the important role that relevant, interesting, and effective visuals play in the intellectual interest of the learner. It does not matter which technologies are used, the content of materials must keep the learner engaged and motivated to use and respond to the information that is being provided. You can use charts, pictures, reference tools, cartoons, videotapes, sound effects—just keep the content interesting and stimulating. In the use of interactive video, the term "edutainment" has been coined for designing materials that learners both enjoy and find beneficial to achieving learning objectives. Use color whenever possible (don't use clear overheads). Use your PC with graphics presentation packages for unique and stimulating presentations. Be sure to keep your graphics simple to make a point, not tell a story. There are excellent resources available to help you design effective visual aids. The *ASTD Handbook of Instructional Technology* (1993) can provide you with fine-tuned details.

Learner to Instructor

The interaction between learner and instructor is such an important factor that we have provided more details on it in Chapter Nineteen, "Train-the-Trainer Preparation." Using the learners' names and knowing who is at each site will help personalize the experience for the participants. In large satellite broadcasts, using learner response pads, the instructor can know who is asking a question and personalize the response. If response pads are not in place, live telephone calls or questions sent to the instructor by fax or e-mail can add to the human-touch link connecting the learner and instructor. During an audio teleconference, learners can introduce themselves and the instructor, who can't see the participants, can use their names to ask questions and stimulate interaction.

Learner to Learner

The importance of interaction among learners is very important to adult learners. There are many ways to stimulate this interaction, once again based on the technologies used. For satellite, you may have the learners meet a half-hour prior to the broadcast to discuss their issues and questions relating to the topic. After the broadcast, you can build in an hour or other designated time for discussions relating to real-world application for the lessons learned. If you are doing computer conferencing, learners can post e-mail questions, engage in an interactive chat line, or interact with one another in any other number of ways.

Earlier we touched on the role of humor in both design and delivery of distance learning courses. Professionals use humor well for on-site courses. Humor becomes especially important if you are using TV as a visual medium for course delivery. Not that you need to have a clown do tricks, but humor can make learning a truly enjoyable experience. Whether you produce a funny videotape to make a point or relate an anecdote—we all have a story or two—that ties into the focus of the learning experience, the key is to creatively think of ways to engage the learner. And life does produce some funny experiences that can be used to tell a story.

Just as instructional designers are the beginning of the course delivery link, the trainers are the ones who will deliver the training and must be a part of the process of course development. Once the trainers are involved, they will be ready to move on to their next step.

Getting ready to teach via distance learning is a process that can be learned. In the next chapter we will share proven ways to learn how to effectively deliver training to remote site learners.

Chapter Nineteen

Train-the-Trainer Preparation

Introduction

It is a fact that trainers play the most important part in the success of any distance learning event. If we look at on-site training, the same fact holds true. Yet, in distance learning, the trainer has a whole new set of skills to learn. These skills are based on understanding and developing a learner-centered mindset, effectively using different technologies, understanding the needs of remote site learners, and integrating continuous interactivity into each course delivered by different distance learning methods.

No one was born with these skills. It's a skill set that can be learned. In this chapter, we want to identify what to do before, during, and after distance learning course delivery. We will cover the key priority areas where you can devote more or less time depending on the experience and skill level of your instructors.

Several important steps are necessary before you will be ready to deliver your courses via distance learning. Let's look at these one step at a time to ensure that the instructors selected for distance learning have the best chance to succeed.

The first place to start is with the current attitudes and mindsets of your instructors. It is common for trainers to resist distance learning. Many instructors want to postpone the 21st century. To start training them without addressing their attitudes, concerns, preconceived notions, and beliefs about distance learning is like decorating a house that has no foundation. This important dimension is typically overlooked as people rush into the how tos. This is a critical first step that should be built into your strategic plan with ways to effectively address both the skills and emotional needs of the instructors. If negative, skeptical, or fearful attitudes are not acknowledged or dealt with, it will be difficult and not very effective to leapfrog to the next part of training. You may be tempted to ignore these attitudes thinking that anyone who has them "will come around later." Don't do it! Deal with them and help the instructors by allowing them to vent their feelings and providing an open forum to express and discuss what is important from their perspective.

By allowing an open dialogue, you can listen and understand why or how they feel the way they do. Their resistance may come from feeling that the training at a distance will not work as well as on site. They may be afraid of using new technologies. No one wants to appear less than proficient to learners, peers, and management, especially if they are seasoned veterans with a track record of success in the classroom. Many instructors are afraid that distance learning may completely replace on-site training. By listening and trying to understand the source of their hesitancy, you will be in a better position to show them how distance learning training, research, and or opportunities can and will address their priority areas of concern.

As described in Chapter One, Karen Mantyla starts every instructor workshop with the following question: "What is the first thing that comes to mind when you hear the words *distance learning?*" The answers from every workshop seem to have common threads of concern. Here are answers called out by both veteran and new training professionals:

"Boring."
"There goes my job."
"Yuck."
"I'll look 10 pounds heavier on TV."
"Impersonal."
"Broadway-like atmosphere."
"No more travel."
"Not as much interaction."
"Lack of classroom control."
"I like the physical presence of learners."
"Talking head."
"Reach more people in a shorter amount of time."

Mantyla's goal is to get the participants' feelings out on the table. Also it is not to be judgmental while listening to them and preparing to address their concerns and perceptions. The goal is to get their attitudes out on the table.

As part of preparing for distance learning, you will want to think about and recommend strategies to help the instructors. Here are some that can be built into your strategic plan:

Conduct an Introductory Workshop for Instructors

This can be done with either internal or external distance learning specialists. Provide opportunities for instructors to have one-on-one guidance to address their individual needs.

Position Distance Learning in All Forms of Communication Methods

Identify and address instructors' most pressing problems. You may use research studies, case studies, or interviews (print, tape, audio) with other instructors who made the transition to distance learning.

Involve Instructors in the Earliest Steps

This could be through discussions, orientations, and active involvement on key teams.

Identify One or Two Enthusiastic Instructors as Leaders

Use these people to start and develop an internal focus group to seek out information, including research, lessons learned and targeted information based on the needs and requirements (both professional and personal) of the training community. Having these open discussions is a wonderful way to gain both knowledge and peer support.

The next step is to explain why an effective distance learning instructor needs a learner-centered mindset, and how to get it. The instructors quoted earlier gave their thoughts about distance learning from their point of view—a natural place to start. Yet because distance learning is measured at the remote sites, the learner will evaluate both the content of the course and the method of delivery. There must be a learner-centered approach to all distance learning initiatives before, during, and after course delivery. Let's start with *before*.

Selecting Instructors

Your initial courses delivered via distance learning will have lots of eyes watching to evaluate its effectiveness—learners, peers, management. The first set of selected courses must be successful because that is where newly minted mindsets about distance learning will be formed. A great outcome will give fuel for allocating more distance learning dollars, increasing learner registrations, and supporting cost-effective options to effectively training your workforce. A failed course will inspire skeptics to conclude that distance learning simply is not good or won't work.

The criteria for the selection of instructors is similar to that of instructional designers but adds one very important criteria—using new technologies. Here's what to look for:

Enthusiasm About Distance Learning

It's important to start with this group. You can convert others at a later time.

Excellent On-Site Instructors

A track record of excellence in delivering on-site training is a basic requirement for distance learning trainers.

Learner-Centered Mindset or Willingness to Develop One

Those who feel very strongly about having an instructor-centered mindset will not be your best candidates.

Flexibility

With new skills to be learned and new technologies being introduced, flexibility is an important attribute. Plus it's a valuable trait for those times when the technology fails and contingency plans are put into effect.

Adaptability

In working with distance learning team members, one way of thinking is often replaced with a collaborative way of designing and delivering the distance learning course.

Sense of Humor

Effective use of humor helps remote site learners enjoy the learning experience.

Willingness to Learn New Technologies

Effective distance learning instructors find out how the equipment works and how to use it to deliver training.

Willingness to Move from a Lecture-based Training

A talking head simply won't be effective, and interaction will be important for each distance learning course.

Willingness to Practice Using Equipment and Rehearse Delivering

Even though instructors may have delivered courses many times, it is important that they practice, practice, and practice before going *live*. Those who don't want to do this should be eliminated from your list of prospective distance learning instructors.

Preparing for Satellite and/or Videoconferencing Delivery

Teaching via distance learning can be delivered by several different delivery systems, as you read in Section Two. Your preparation is determined by the method of delivery that you will be using. For our purposes here, we will help you prepare for what are now the most popular methods of delivery, namely, satellite (one-way video, two-way audio) and videoconferencing (two-way video, two-way audio).

Visual Aids

Delivery via satellite or videoconferencing is most effective with excellent visualizations for the remote site learners, so work in tandem with your instructional designers on the visual aids. People get into a TV mentality and expect the same kind of interesting and high-quality visuals that they get with that medium. The visuals you can use include the following:

Graphic slides from your PC. You can design a graphic presentation and deliver it via your PC directly into the TV feed. This technology allows you the flexibility to create interesting and customized "slides" that can be changed (if necessary) with last-minute, late-breaking information! Or you can prepare viewgraphs and display them with your pictures or three-dimensional objects below.

Some rules of thumb: Visuals help focus remote site learners on key learning points. These visuals should not be text heavy (you can put those with a lot of text in your remote site material packet). They should be in a horizontal format for the TV-screen type of viewing. They should be in color and have no more than six bullets down and no more than six words across. A clip art graphic or two adds interest, but don't crowd the visual with too many. Use illustrations such as bar graphs in lieu of text wherever possible. Rules of thumb for illustrations: Keep those visuals eye-appealing and simple. Use dark letters against a light background or light letters against a dark background. Use 36-point to 42-point type for titles and a minimum of 24-point to 30-point type for text. Use upper and lower case for emphasis. Sans-Serif fonts (without feet e.g. arial) work best with visuals. You may choose to include a copy of your slides (black and white copies are fine) in your predistributed handout package. If you have a Web home page, you can have remote site coordinators download your slides for distribution at each remote site.

Videotapes. These can be effectively used to show a role-model example of your teaching points and help achieve learning objectives. Rule of thumb: Show videotapes in segments that last no more than 10 minutes. Do not show a 20-minute videotape straight through. You will lose your remote site learners. Show segmented clips and build in interactive exercises or Q&A after each segment.

Pictures or three-dimensional objects. Most origination sites (where you will be delivering the training) have a document camera. This camera has a zoom feature that allows your to show fine detail on pictures, and it has the capacity to demonstrate the use of a three-dimensional object. One distance learning instructor used a laptop computer under the document camera to show remote site learners how to use a trackball! The ability to use live motion coupled with objects is a wonderful addition to your toolbox.

Interaction Activities

As we noted in Chapter Eighteen's discussion about instructional design, it is vital to build interactivity into each distance learning course. The rule of thumb from both distance educators and trainers is to build in creative and engaging interactive activities every five to seven minutes. The Interactivity Guide Pyramid and the Interactivity Spectrum shown on the next two pages can help you develop and deliver a well-balanced program.

Balancing interaction activity choices. How can you design for a "well-balanced" selection of program activities? Just as the Food Guide Pyramid can help you make wise food choices, the Interactivity Guide Pyramid on the next page can help you make wise choices for your program. For example, choose

3-5 servings of activities	from the **Personalize Group**
3-4 servings of activities	from the **Participate Group**
2-3 servings of activities	from the **Show Group**
3-5 servings of activities	from the **Question Group**
sparingly	from the **Presentation Group (if one-way presentation)** and use more generously if mixed with activities from the other groups.

The compressed video environment logically leads to an emphasis on interaction. Interactivity can involve participants at remote sites during sessions and off site for individual and group projects and communication. Interaction activities

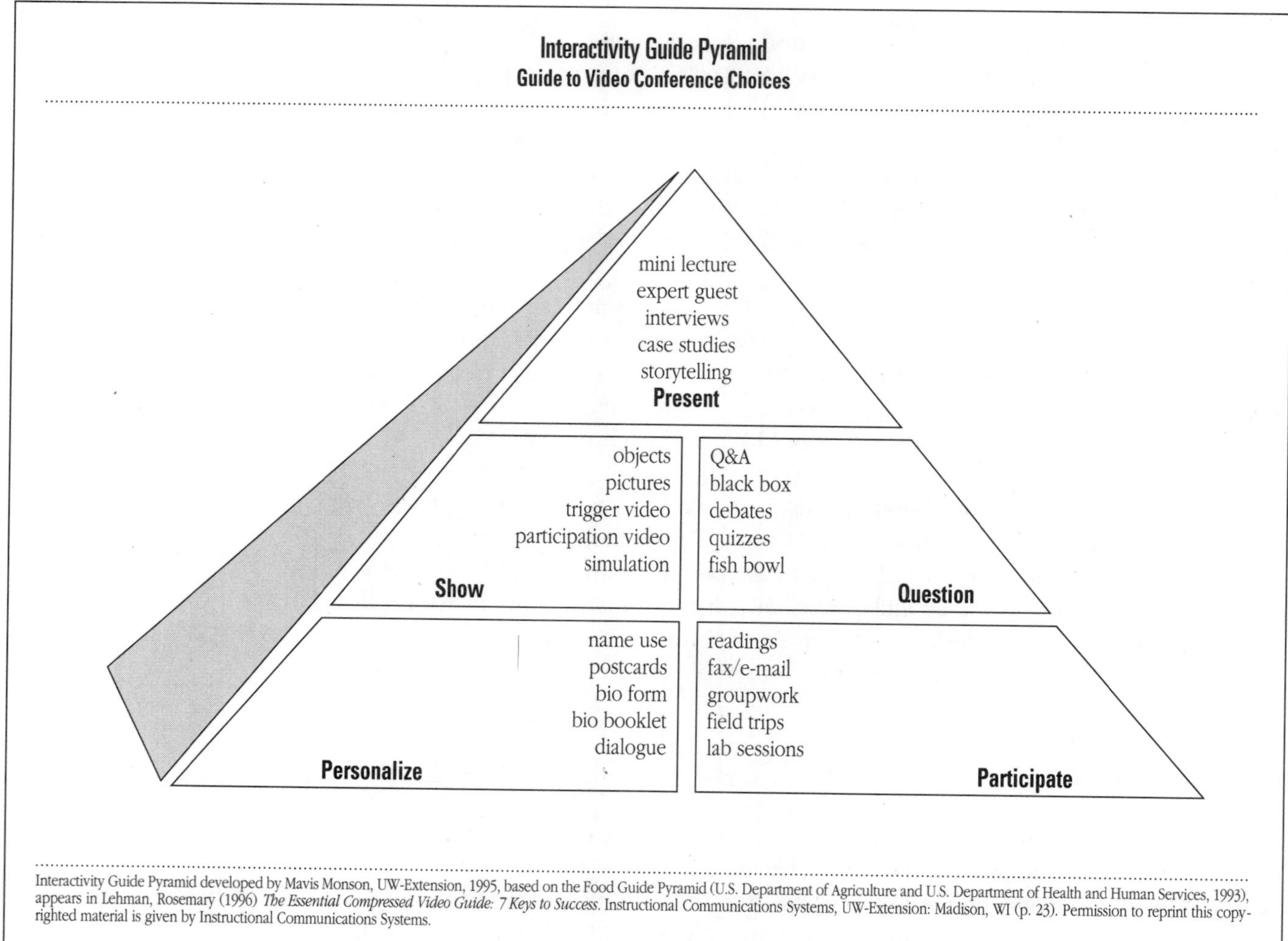

Interactivity Guide Pyramid developed by Mavis Monson, UW-Extension, 1995, based on the Food Guide Pyramid (U.S. Department of Agriculture and U.S. Department of Health and Human Services, 1993), appears in Lehman, Rosemary (1996) *The Essential Compressed Video Guide: 7 Keys to Success*. Instructional Communications Systems, UW-Extension: Madison, WI (p. 23). Permission to reprint this copyrighted material is given by Instructional Communications Systems.

should be short, intense, well-planned, match with objectives, and be meaningful, enjoyable, involving, and shareable. Interactivity spans the spectrum from single to complex and includes strategies to present, personalize, show, participate, and question. The Interactivity Spectrum on the next page lists 25 activities categorized according to these strategies.

Appearance

Because TV is a visual medium, you are the first visual the remote site learners will see. Your appearance is important. Wear conservative clothing and use plain or muted patterns. Shades of navy, green, blue, and gray work best. Avoid white because it glares. Remove excess jewelry and pocket items that may jingle!

Equipment

Become familiar with the equipment that you will be using. Have your technical experts arrange for vendors to provide training on their equipment well in advance of delivering your course. A major key to the success of delivery will be the confi-

Interactivity Spectrum
(from simple to complex)

Present	Personalize	Show	Participate	Question
mini lecture	name use	objects	readings	Q&A
expert guest(s)	postcards	pictures	fax/e-mail	black box
interviews	bio form	trigger video	groupwork	debates
case study	bio booklet	participation video	field trips	quizzes
storytelling	dialogue	simulation	lab sessions	fish bowl

Interactivity Spectrum developed by Rosemary Lehman, UW-Extension, 1995, appears in Lehman, Rosemary (1996), *The Essential Compressed Video Guide: 7 Keys to Success*. Instructional Communications Systems, UW-Extension: Madison, WI (p. 19). Permission to reprint this copyrighted material is given by Instructional Communications Systems.

dence you exhibit while delivering your course. It can't be said enough: Practice using the equipment several times, and do at least two rehearsals prior to going "live." If you feel confident, you will do a better job. Practice as many times as you need to in order to feel comfortable. You also want to be well versed on the equipment used at the remote sites.

Pre-Course Administration

You want to be sure to utilize all possible communication methods (print based, local area network, wide area network, etc.) to reach your target audience. Determine the time frame for scheduling communication efforts in order to reach the greatest number of targeted participants. Identify the point of contact for registrations, local assessments, and evaluations. You need to clearly define who does what. Prepare your course registration process and forms. Design a welcome visual that will "greet" the remote site learners when they enter the room. It can have your logo, the name of the course, and other details specific to your course.

Course Preliminaries

Arrive at least 30 minutes prior to the course. Welcome the participants with a big smile. (Your initial enthusiasm and smile will go a long way—literally!) Start the interactions early by using someone's name or site. Based on the number of sites, you can have different people introduce themselves or do a roll call visually by site.

Let participants know if you are audiotaping or videotaping the course and that you will explain how to get copies at the end of the program. Explain the course logistics, such as if and when you will have two 15-minute breaks, one in 45 minutes and another in two hours. Succinctly review how to use the equipment at the remote sites. Note that the remote site participant packets should have a one-page overview on the equipment available and how to use it.

Presentation Delivery

Look directly at the camera. Maintain good eye contact with the lens (the "eyes" of the participants). Speak with a normal voice and use inflections whenever possible. Smile, smile, smile!

Question and Answer Sessions

Establish ground rules prior to course delivery. Note that these should be enclosed in the remote site participant packets. For satellite delivered courses, the learners may be using learner response pads, a telephone for live call-ins, or a fax machine, or a combination of these. For video teleconferencing, learners should wait until someone has finished talking. Each learner should give his or her name and site location. If you find that learners are reluctant to ask questions, you can encourage comments and learner interactions by asking for comments on a graphic.

Participation

It is easier to manage remote site participation with satellite delivery than with video teleconferencing because you decide when to call on a remote learner, read a question, or take a call. With video teleconferencing, learners can ask or answer questions without waiting for your cue. Remember the Unisys case study? The instructor went from an average single-site classroom of 25 learners to over 1,000 learners. Participation was easily handled with the learner response pads and host controller system. If you have a point-to-point (one site to another site) video teleconference, it will be easier to handle participation than with a multi-point call (your site to multiple sites). Plan for whatever delivery medium you may be using to help effectively manage participation.

Contingency Plans

When we use technology for any reason, we have to build in "Plan B" or "Plan C" in case something goes wrong. If you have difficulty with your video picture, explain the situation to the participants and continue to deliver your course with the audio. However, if your course depends on visualization, you may want to wait a few minutes while the technical staff tries to fix the problem. You can use some audio interactions to keep the learners engaged. If you should have difficulties with the audio portion, use your document camera to send a note to the remote sites.

When you have either video or audio difficulties, update the participants every two or three minutes. Don't leave them wondering what's going on. If problems persist, end the session and let the learners that you will notify them of a reschedule date.

Course Endings

List any actions, post-course homework, or follow-up expected from the learners. You should prepare visuals in advance of the session for any required work. If you have planned any remote site discussions for after the session, specify what you would like them to accomplish.

Provide learners with post-course support methods of communication that they might need for questions or individual guidance. This "help line" can also be done in a visual format and shown on the screen prior to your last visual. See Chapter Twenty-Three, "Learner Support System Design," for ideas on how to support your remote learners. Ask the learners to complete the evaluation form and provide directions on either mailing it directly to you or giving it to your remote site facilitator.

In this chapter, we have provided an overview of the key result areas that you need to address to prepare trainers to teach at a distance. There are courses, schools, and specialized training programs specifically designed to train the distance learning trainers. A list of training providers appears in Appendix A. Be sure to match your training requirements with providers that specialize in the technologies that you will use for your distance learning system.

The goal for each learner is to achieve the learning objectives and enjoy the learning experience. Our chapter on remote site coordination can help support the achievement of that goal.

CHAPTER TWENTY

Remote Site Materials Preparation and Development

INTRODUCTION

The success of distance learning is measured at the remote sites. Everything that is done for and with the remote site learners will be evaluated by them. If the learners are not satisfied with any aspects of the learning experience, they will form judgments, mindsets, and expectations about future distance learning events. To make the best first impression, remote site materials must be designed for each course or event. This chapter contains information about

- why remote site materials are so important
- what well-prepared materials will do for the learners
- how trainers can effectively use these materials
- how to create effective remote site materials.

WHY REMOTE SITE MATERIALS ARE SO IMPORTANT

By the time you are ready to prepare your own materials, you have attended distance learning events. Most likely, you were given some type of material or packet when you walked in or out of the door at those events. Our first impression of what we see is often formed in the first seven seconds of contact with either materials or people! That's an important point to remember as we begin to look at the first impression you want learners to make.

Distance learners must have all the support tools necessary to both enjoy the learning experience and benefit from participating in the learning experience. The fact that the learner is participating in a new way of learning means that we must often take extra time to think about what is important from their perspective.

WHAT WELL-PREPARED MATERIALS WILL DO FOR THE LEARNERS

The learners want to know and feel the following:

- Distance learning is an exciting way to learn! (A motivated learner is invaluable!)

- Distance learning is a first-class method of learning and as good (or better) than learning on site! (It's not a second-class experience.)

- The course was designed with objectives that will help them achieve professional or personal success, or both. The content applies to their work and provides opportunities for skill development.
- They understand what to expect and how it will work. (They are not confused.)
- They have an easy-to-use guide on how to use the equipment. (They'll be able to concentrate on the learning experience, not on how to use the technology.)
- They know how they are expected to participate in the learning event. (They know how to ask questions, make comments, and be an important part of the learning experience.)
- They know where to turn for help or guidance after the event. (They don't want to be left hanging.)
- The instructor is excited and enthusiastic about delivering the training. (They will sense your enthusiasm or the lack of it—it will be contagious either way.)

The learners' expectations form the basis of how we need to work with our instructional design team in creating remote site materials. These materials become the "silent partner" for you, the trainer. They position your course as an active learning event and you as an instructor who encourages and expects participation from every learner. You make each person feel important. As a further support, the contents you provide will include learning and application tools and information that learners can use as a self-directed learning resources after the course is delivered.

How Trainers Can Effectively Use These Materials

The materials can and will serve to support your success by

- communicating excitement about this new way of learning
- telling learners how to use the equipment. (This will allow for the seamless use of technology to deliver the training. You want to have the learners focus on the content and not on the delivery method.)
- providing subject content information that can also be used as a self-directed learning resource after the training event
- offering application guidelines. (They can provide information on how learners can apply the lessons learned to work or personal situations.)
- including interactivity tools, exercises, and methods for use during and after the live event
- providing information on how to receive further guidance or help with individ-

ual questions and needs.

With the careful development of your remote site material packet, you can provide everything that is in this list.

How to Create Effective Remote Site Materials

The first impression we want to make is one of professionalism. We want the remote site learners to know that they are about to participate in a first-class learning event and that we took the time to create excellent support materials. We know how we feel when something looks like it was carefully prepared. It gives more meaning and says, "This is important." The following tips will guide you as you develop your own participant packets:

Packet "Packaging"

The first impression will be made by the appearance of all material in the participants' packet. Appearance here is just as important as your professional image in front of a camera. Learners will first see the outer covering of the materials so the packet should be in a professional folder or customized binder. You may want to design a logo for your distance learning program that can be used for any course materials. The "look" of this logo can be your trademark for all distance learning communication and marketing vehicles.

Learner Welcome Letter

Each packet should have a welcome letter that is addressed to the learner. This letter could include the following:

- the name of the course, date, time, and location of the distance learning event
- pre-course assignments, such as reading requirements
- a list of items that are contained in the packet
- a closing statement that encourages the learner to participate in the learning event through comments and questions
- the name and telephone number of the person to call in the event the learner has questions prior to the event.

Additional Resource Materials Listing

Include a list of resource materials for pre- and post-course readings. This information can be valuable in supporting a learner's ability to accomplish learning objectives. A learner may want or need further informational guidance on the subject, and this can be a guide to stimulate self-directed learning initiatives.

Interactive Workbook and Study Guide

This workbook is often the core vehicle to provide learners with detailed subject content information (to support the key points in your course) copies of any slides that you may use during the course (numbered so that the learners can quickly turn to the right one), specific readings, case studies, and the all-important interactive exercises.

The interactive strategies that you and your team build into your course design should be varied and fun. (See page 118 to refer to the Interactivity Guide Pyramid and page 119 to refer to the Interactivity Spectrum.) The amount and type of activities you choose will be determined in large part by the technologies you use (audio, one- or two-way video, etc.) and by the level of participation desired throughout your course. Once again, it is important to number pages, slides, and exercises so that everyone can find them quickly. If you are using television, the visual medium should be used to help maximize the learning activities.

Interactive word pictures, word scramble, games, video clips, pictures, and the like are excellent ways to visually communicate the activity and stimulate learner participation. There are many excellent distance learning resources that devote entire books to interactivity exercises, and several are listed in Appendix C.

Instruction Sheet

Include an instruction sheet explaining how to use any technologies necessary for this course. The key here is to keep the explanation simple, short, and to the point, and to provide a telephone number or hot line learners can call if they need help using the equipment. Explain what is in the room, how it works, how the learner can use it, and what benefits it provides.

Ground Rules

Explain the ground rules of how the course will be conducted and provide guidelines about how and when to ask questions, make comments, and interact with the trainer. If the equipment that you use for distance learning includes a learner response pad system, include a simple explanation of how it works.

Course Agenda

Use time notations for the start of each segment of the course and briefly list what will be covered in each time frame. If you have a course that requires one or more breaks, list when they are and for how long. Don't forget to include breaks in your agenda! Be sure to remind learners that it is critical to return on time.

Course Description

Here's where you want to detail:

- importance of the course for learners
- what they are to learn

- overview of the content
- homework assignments, reports, or projects to be done and due dates
- pertinent information about the trainer and his or her credentials.

Provide this information in a step-by-step fashion, just as we have listed above. It's easier for learners to understand it on their own when instructors explain it in bite-size pieces.

Roster of Participants

Learners like to know who else is taking a course. A list of all learners (or remote sites) is a nice way of letting them know their peers in different parts of the country or world. If you have a large satellite broadcast with hundreds or thousands of learners, list the site locations. People like to see their name in distance learning materials. Once again, it is a learner-centered way of thinking to make them feel important in your virtual classroom.

Evaluation Form

This tool, which is covered in more detail in Chapter Twenty-Two, should be enclosed in the remote site material packet. It should be easy to understand and clearly allow the learner to evaluate both the content and method(s) of delivery. Instructions on where to send the form should also be included. If your remote site facilitator will collect evaluation forms, note that in the instructions.

The importance of proper preparation of remote site materials can't be overemphasized. It is with these materials that learners' distance learning mindset will begin.

Chapter Twenty-One

Remote Site Coordination

Introduction

You've worked hard to design and develop your distance learning course, and you want to take every necessary step to support its success. Effective remote site coordination is a critical component of your distance learning strategic plan and a step you don't want to miss. It is a logical step to take because success for distance learning is measured at the remote sites. It makes good sense to focus on how to get excellent evaluations for both course content and a new way of learning.

In this chapter, we will discuss the importance of site coordination and provide guidelines on how to select and define the role for your site coordinators. We will also provide tips for conducting remote site activities to support and enhance the achievement of learning objectives coupled with ways to create an enjoyable learning environment.

Effective local site coordination is significant for

- learners
- instructors
- distance learning course success.

Let's take a look at each of these areas and see how effective site coordination and support will increase the success for your distance learning initiatives.

Coordination priorities include providing technical, administrative, and instructional support for each remote site location. Careful preparation begins with defining the role of your site coordinators, identifying the skills they need, selecting those that best fit the profile needed for this position, and training them in key result areas.

Learner Considerations

Let's start with the learners and what they want and need when they walk into the distance learning classroom:

- a warm and enthusiastic welcome. (Distance learners are sometimes skeptical about this new way of learning.)

- physical comfort in the classroom. (Learners want rooms that aren't crowded, have comfortable temperatures and comfortable chairs, and let them see the TV monitor clearly.)

- knowledge of how the course will be conducted. (They have a feeling of confidence knowing what to expect.)

- knowledge of the equipment in the classroom and how to use it. (They feel more at ease when they understand what equipment they will use and how it works.)

- how to interact in the learning environment. (Distance learners want to know what to do if they have questions, problems, or comments.)

- understanding of the learning environment and objectives

- logistics for taking breaks.

Imagine yourself as a learner, walking into a distance learning classroom and having no one there to guide you through what you need to know. It would be hard to concentrate on learning. Effective remote site coordination will allow your learners to concentrate on the learning experience, not the technology.

Coordinator Considerations

A well trained site coordinator is a tremendous asset to the trainer. In defining the role for site coordinators, here are some responsibilities you want to consider in varying degrees, based on the size and requirements of different sites:

- creating a good learning environment: facilities have proper seating and work areas for pre-, live-, and post-program activities; comfortable lighting and temperature; and reduction in noises or activities outside of the room to eliminate distractions

- helping participants feel comfortable: warm welcome at the door; name tags ready; sufficient time scheduled to explain how everything will work (not a rushed five minutes before airtime); enough time before broadcast to answer questions about logistics, local facilities (such as restrooms, snack areas, and telephones), and participation during the program; explanation of your role and what you will do to help facilitate the learning experience

- preparing for learning: review of any pre-course handouts to be sure that everyone has a complete package; learning objectives highlighted; description of the different ways to participate based on the equipment at the remote site; discussion of planned group activities at the local site before and after the live event

- explaining technical support: orientations for learners on use of the equipment; whom to call in case of technical difficulties and technical needs; equipment in working order prior to course delivery; assistance for learners on equipment use when needed

- managing administrative details: handle local registrations; material distribution; preparation of roster; proctoring of tests during the program; collection of evaluations and assessments; fax questions from remote sites to instructors; review preprogram checklist of items to be completed before, during, and after the program covering all administrative, technical, environmental, and instruction information needed to support the learners and instructor; ensure that the technical point of contact will be available to help address any needs the day of the program; up-to-date telephone, e-mail, fax numbers for the technical and instructor (origination site) locations.

These responsibilities provide an overview of the most common support responsibilities for effective remote site coordination. You may require more, less, or different responsibilities. The goal is to ensure that you build this support into your strategic plan as an important part of your whole distance learning system.

The importance of effective site coordination is often overlooked. Those who have started distance learning say that this area often receives insufficient resources in the budgeting and planning process. From the hard lessons learned, we know that we must ensure that the local site is equipped not only with the equipment but also with the support needed to achieve successful learning outcomes—from both sides of the lens.

Often site coordinators have another job, and site coordination activities are given to someone as a part of the overall job responsibilities. When distance learning course delivery increases, there may be a need for a full-time coordinator. Part-time or full time, here are the qualities you want in the site coordinators you select:

- caring
- nurturing
- enthusiastic about distance learning
- excellent communication skills
- detail minded
- flexible
- adaptable
- sense of humor.

These qualities are very important at the remote sites. It is important to select people who won't look at this role as an annoyance but will consider it important. They will see the coordinator as a key member who has a stake in the successful outcome of the learning experience. The coordinator can have the power to influence, positively or negatively, the extent to which learners feel satisfaction and achievement from the event and whether they have confidence in learning. That's a powerful statement and one that should be taken seriously in the selection of site coordinators.

A frequently asked question about site coordinators is, "Do they need to have subject matter expertise?" The answer varies depending on whom you talk to. There have been very successful distance learning evaluations with a site coordinator who knows how to facilitate the learning experience and guide the learners to getting their questions answered by the instructor but doesn't necessarily have subject matter expertise. There have also been coordinators who know the general content of the subject. It would be foolish to assume that every site coordinator needs to be a content expert in the subject being taught.

Another frequently asked question is, "Should a learner enrolled in the course be tasked to be the site coordinator?" Our experience shows that learners should not be expected to do this job. They are there to learn with undivided attention. They may think it would be fun—and it would—but that's not why they are in the classroom. The most important role of the coordinator is to help support the effectiveness of the learning experience. That's the bottom line.

Coordinator Training

As with any position of importance to the success of your program, you not only want to define the responsibilities and interview to select the right candidates, but you also want to design and deliver a training program to provide a solid foundation for success. It may seem bizarre to be telling training professionals that they must provide training to the site coordinator. However, lessons learned show that no training equals lack of coordination, confusion, and less than successful learning outcomes.

You can design a training program that identifies the responsibilities of the position and illustrates how to do it. You may decide to train at a distance! This way would help you not only train but also ensure that your coordinators know how to use the technical equipment. You can prepare a simple remote site coordinator's guide as a reference for easy access. Provide both initial training and develop ongoing feedback and contact systems to help motivate and empower your site coordinators.

Now that we know that we have provided support for the remote site learners, we will move on to helping to identify the key factors needed to successfully measure the effectiveness of the learning experience. These key measurement tools will not only help validate the learning outcomes but also focus on evaluating the method of delivery, as judged by the learners.

CHAPTER TWENTY-TWO

Course Evaluation Tool Development

INTRODUCTION

Many trainers often ask the question, "What's the difference between developing evaluation tools for distance learning versus those for on-site courses?" Evaluations in distance learning usually focus not only on learner comprehension and retention but also the instructional process itself. Did the learners enjoy or hate the training? Did they hate it? Were they sleeping at the remote sites because they were bored, flying paper airplanes across the room because you couldn't see? Will the participants actually perform their jobs better because of the training they've received? What areas get good and bad evaluations in distance learning?

As a training professional, you understand the purpose and importance of evaluation. You most likely have developed evaluation tools and methods that are used to answer these questions for your on-site courses. Our goal is not to review the value and importance of evaluation, nor to stress the theories that validate the need for evaluation. The purpose of this chapter is to answer the question, "What do I need to know about evaluating the effectiveness of delivering training via distance learning methods?" We will identify the key result areas for distance learning evaluation and provide actual tools used by two organizations to measure the effectiveness of their distance learning courses. As the saying goes, "A picture is worth a thousand words." You'll see a clear picture of two tools that help both organizations effectively evaluate their distance learning environment from the perspective of the learner.

In this chapter we will describe

- key evaluation areas for distance learning
- types of evaluation methods used
- evaluation tools
- lessons learned in developing evaluation tools.

KEY EVALUATION AREAS FOR DISTANCE LEARNING

When you begin your distance learning journey, and as you continue to develop your programs, work in a collaborative fashion with team members for different functional areas. Each person is naturally interested in the evaluation for the desired end result (successful training outcomes) but is also very interested in and requires feedback for his or her specific area of operation. The finance person may first look at the cost-effectiveness of the delivery; the instructional designers will want to know how the ISD model they used worked for the instructor and learners; the learners want to see if they will like this new way of learning; and the instructors want to see how they liked it and did it work. From all eyes in the organization, distance learning will be judged for both the process of learning the content and the methods of training delivery.

Your organization as a whole may have a philosophy of evaluation that will serve as a guide in developing your evaluation tools. There are defined purposes for your evaluation methods and models, and specific information that may be required by decision makers. You most likely have existing evaluation systems that could be modified to include specifics needed for distance learning courses, especially for interactive television delivery.

Your evaluation tools should focus on measuring learning outcomes, making improvements, planning future actions, and analyzing the cost-effectiveness of course delivery. The key content areas to include in your evaluations are as follows:

Learner and Instructor Satisfaction

How satisfied was the learner in the following:

- achieving learning objectives
- enjoying the learning experience
- knowing how to apply the subject content to work and to personal applications
- feeling comfortable asking questions
- getting answers to those questions
- being comfortable in the learning environment
- understanding how to use the technology
- participating in an active learning experience
- being able to use supporting materials in an easy-to-use, self-directed format
- getting support from the site facilitator.

How satisfied was the instructor in the following:

- feeling comfortable using the technology
- feeling comfortable with the instructional design of the course
- achieving the goals of the program
- enjoying the teaching experience
- utilizing different multimedia tools during instruction
- being able to actively engage the learners at different remote sites
- being able to use interactive strategies and exercises every five to seven minutes
- assessing the learners' ability to understand and apply learning content
- teaching via this method of distance learning.

How cost-effective was the program in the following:

- reducing the amount of dollars spent on travel (this method compared with historical information on the on-site delivery method)
- reducing the amount of time needed to travel to receive instruction (travel between learner origination points and on-site destination points based on historical information)
- the number of learners trained at one time (e.g., 25 learners on site compared with 1,000 via satellite delivery)
- the cost per participant (total distance learning delivery costs divided by the number of learners)
- the cost per participant of on-site delivery of this course compared with distance learning methods of delivery.

You may want to include additional categories of evaluation to meet your or your organization's specific requirements or quality standards.

Types of Evaluation Methods Used

There are several different methods that you may want to utilize based on your needs and the availability of resources. The most common ones include

- learner feedback forms (see pages 137–140 for sample forms)
- instructor feedback forms
- site facilitator feedback forms
- focus groups of learners conducted via the delivery method used
- telephone interviews with learners, instructors, and facilitators
- cost-benefit analysis worksheet completed for each course delivered via different methods of training delivery.

Whichever methods you use choose, the responses must satisfy the following questions:

- What is the purpose of the evaluation for our organization?
- Which aspects of distance learning are important to evaluate?
- How will we define and measure success?
- What methods of evaluation will work best for us?
- How will we analyze the evaluation results?
- How will we use the results?

Evaluation Tools

Two examples of active evaluation tools that the Unisys Corporation and the U.S. Air Force use are found beginning on page 137. Let's take a look at them and visualize the key factors included for distance learning course delivery.

Unisys Corporation

The Unisys model includes the following:

General information to provide you with a learner profile. This type of information is valuable for instructors as they prepare courses and learner support systems. Based on the type of job and the learner's experience, the instructor will be in a better position to provide meaningful guidance.

Broadcast information to measure the satisfaction with the learning environment, method of delivery, and motivation to attend future distance learning courses. Based on the answers to these questions, future sessions can be enhanced by uncovering the reasons for the rating and strengthening any area or areas that received a less than favorable response.

Post-broadcast session evaluation. This evaluation is a terrific way to help measure motivation and the value of the self-directed course materials. If the learners feel good in the learning environment, they will be more motivated to apply the lessons learned. This is true of all learning, yet becomes even more critical when the instructor can't be physically there to help the learner. Self-directed motivation for the learner is an important aspect to remember in all aspects of design, delivery, and support systems.

The measurement of productivity gains noted in the sample on page 138 (questions 14 to 16) help to achieve level-4 evaluation outcomes. This self-assessment section reflected what each learner actually felt about the lessons learned as applied to his or her own job situation.

United States Air Force

Now we'll look at an evaluation tool utilized by the U.S. Air Force for a very technical training course delivered by using satellite (see pages 139–140). The satellite method of delivery is called video teletraining, or VTT. The goal of this model is to measure learner satisfaction in several key areas.

You've heard us say several times throughout the book that the success of distance learning is measured at the remote sites by the learners. This tool is designed to evaluate the satisfaction quotient of the following aspects of the distance learning course:

Classroom environment. Starting with the learners' comfort, these 12 questions will help the distance learning team focus on the environmental issues that are most important to remote site participants.

Instructor. A critical look at the measurement factors that are important from the perspective of the learner. Continuous process improvement from the instructors podium can be achieved with honest and direct feedback from the remote sites.

Site monitor or facilitator. This is a good evaluation method to see if the person helped the learners achieve the desired level of support needed to facilitate the learning process.

UNISYS

DESKTOP IDL EVALUATION
For Word for Windows 6.0–Program 6

SITE LOCATION____

ORG. NAME ________________________ **NAME (OPTIONAL)** ________________

Your input is extremely valuable in assisting us to evaluate the effectiveness of this program. Please read each statement carefully and circle the appropriate response. When complete, double fold this sheet on the dotted line with the return address exposed. Staple and return using Unisys interoffice mail.

General Information

A. Please match your job to the closest category provided.

Manager/Supervisor | Technical/Professional | Administrative Professional
Direct Sales | Non-Exempt Technical | Non-Exempt Admin./Clerical
Non-Exempt Other

B. What (if anything) keeps you from using your PC to effectively perform you job responsibilities? (Choose all that apply)

Lack of time | Lack of training | No management support for training
Inadequate hardware | Inadequate software | Other:________________

C. Assess your current knowledge of Word for Windows 6.0.

Novice | Intermediate | Expert

Broadcast Session Evaluation

	Strongly Agree				Strongly Disagree
1. This session was time well spent in discovering practical and useful ideas and techniques.	5	4	3	2	1
2. The length of the session (1 hour) is appropriate.	5	4	3	2	1
3. The facilitator(s) presented the material in a clear and understanding manner.	5	4	3	2	1
4. Questions I had during the broadcast were answered.	5	4	3	2	1

5. Did you find this session informative?	Yes	No	Undecided
6. Did you learn something useful during this session?	Yes	No	Undecided
7. Will you attend the next program session?	Yes	No	Undecided
8. Would you recommend this course to others?	Yes	No	Undecided

continued on next page

UNISYS **INTEROFFICE MAIL**

Please return this evaluation to:

Attention: Mary McAdoo

Location: Blue Bell

To return: Double fold using this dotted line, with above address exposed, and staple.

Post-Broadcast Session Evaluation:
Please complete the follow questions after using the exercises, CBT, and/or references.

	Strongly Agree				Strongly Disagree
9. I was motivated by the program to complete the exercises at my desk.	5	4	3	2	1
10. The materials were well designed to complement the session presentation.	5	4	3	2	1
11. The exercises helped to reinforce my learning on each topic.	5	4	3	2	1
12. The CBT, include with the package, helped to reinforce my learning on each topic.	5	4	3	2	1
13. The references to the QUE book, CBT, and On-Line HELP were a valuable part of the program.	5	4	3	2	1

14. What percent of your total working time will be spent on tasks that require the skill/knowledge presented in the course? (Circle one)

0 10 20 30 40 50 60 70 80 90 100

15. Rate your productivity, **before** this learning experience, on your job tasks that required the skill/knowledge presented in the course (100 percent represents highest productivity; 50 percent means that you could complete the tasks half as well, or half as fast).

0 10 20 30 40 50 60 70 80 90 100

16. Rate your productivity, (future project) **after** this learning experience, on your job tasks that require the skills/knowledge presented in the course (100 percent represents highest productivity; 50 percent means that you could complete the tasks half as well, or half as fast).

0 10 20 30 40 50 60 70 80 90 100

STUDENT CRITIQUE
VIDEO TELETRAINING (VTT)

COURSE TITLE			PDS CODE
KC-135R QUICK START AUXILIARY POWER UNIT SYSTEM (QSAS)			5P8
COURSE NUMBER	TRAINING LOCATION		GRADUATION DATE
J6ADL2A6X1A-027			
NAME (OPTIONAL)	DSN PHONE (OPTIONAL)	RESPONSE REQUIRED YES/NO	EXPERIENCE (CIRCLE ONE) 1. LESS THAN 2 YEARS 2. 2-5YEARS 3. MORE THAN 5 YEARS

SAMPLE LAYOUT

Please give us your opinion regarding this video teletraining (VTT) session. We will use your comments to improve future televised courses. Respond honestly and objectively. We appreciate any constructive criticism you can give us. Please tell us how we can teach this course more effectively. Return the completed forms to your site monitor. Thanks!

INSTRUCTIONS: Read each statement below. Circle the option which best identifies your opinion of the statement.

How satisfied are you with the...?	Not at all satisfied								Extremely satisfied	Not applicable
1. CLASSROOM ENVIRONMENT										
a. Operation of the classroom equipment	1	2	3	4	5	6	7	8	9	0
b. Quality of audio reception	1	2	3	4	5	6	7	8	9	0
c. Quality of video reception	1	2	3	4	5	6	7	8	9	0
d. Number of microphones in the classroom	1	2	3	4	5	6	7	8	9	0
e. Size of the presentation monitor(s)	1	2	3	4	5	6	7	8	9	0
f. Location of the presentation monitor(s)	1	2	3	4	5	6	7	8	9	0
g. Appropriateness of break schedules and break times	1	2	3	4	5	6	7	8	9	0
h. Length of the lunch break	1	2	3	4	5	6	7	8	9	0
i. Length of the course	1	2	3	4	5	6	7	8	9	0
j. Length of training day	1	2	3	4	5	6	7	8	9	0
k. Time allocated for study and reading activities	1	2	3	4	5	6	7	8	9	0
l. Overall learning atmosphere	1	2	3	4	5	6	7	8	9	0
2. INSTRUCTOR										
a. Knowledge of the course material	1	2	3	4	5	6	7	8	9	0
b. Interaction with students	1	2	3	4	5	6	7	8	9	0
c. Ability to keep the interest of the class	1	2	3	4	5	6	7	8	9	0
d. Control of the rate and pace of instruction	1	2	3	4	5	6	7	8	9	0
e. Television image and professional appearance	1	2	3	4	5	6	7	8	9	0
f. Gestures, mannerisms and eye contact	1	2	3	4	5	6	7	8	9	0
g. Poise, confidence and enthusiasm	1	2	3	4	5	6	7	8	9	0
h. Responsiveness to student questions and problems	1	2	3	4	5	6	7	8	9	0

continued on next page

How satisfied are you with the...?	Not at all satisfied								Extremely satisfied	Not applicable
3. SITE MONITOR										
a. Instructions provided (I knew what was expected of me.)	1	2	3	4	5	6	7	8	9	0
b. Comfort with equipment	1	2	3	4	5	6	7	8	9	0
c. Explanation of operation of microphones	1	2	3	4	5	6	7	8	9	0
d. Ability to resolve audio/video problems	1	2	3	4	5	6	7	8	9	0
e. Responsiveness to student questions and problems	1	2	3	4	5	6	7	8	9	0
f. Overall quality of site monitor's request	1	2	3	4	5	6	7	8	9	0
4. COURSE CONTENT										
a. Sequence of topics	1	2	3	4	5	6	7	8	9	0
b. Communication of objectives in clear, understandable terms	1	2	3	4	5	6	7	8	9	0
c. Relevance of course content to the job	1	2	3	4	5	6	7	8	9	0
d. Ease of applying what you've learned to the job	1	2	3	4	5	6	7	8	9	0
e. Use of questions to encourage active student involvement	1	2	3	4	5	6	7	8	9	0
f. Use of questions to enhance learning	1	2	3	4	5	6	7	8	9	0
g. Time provided to answer student questions	1	2	3	4	5	6	7	8	9	0
h. Use of summaries to review main points	1	2	3	4	5	6	7	8	9	0
i. Course's emphasis on the most important information	1	2	3	4	5	6	7	8	9	0
j. Presentation of technical information	1	2	3	4	5	6	7	8	9	0
k. Emphasis on safety procedures during the course	1	2	3	4	5	6	7	8	9	0
5. MEDIA										
a. Classroom materials received at your site	1	2	3	4	5	6	7	8	9	0
b. Relevance of visuals to instruction	1	2	3	4	5	6	7	8	9	0
c. Clearness and appearance of visuals	1	2	3	4	5	6	7	8	9	0
d. Availability of technical publications/regulations	1	2	3	4	5	6	7	8	9	0
e. Use of training aids	1	2	3	4	5	6	7	8	9	0
6. TESTING										
a. Testing environment	1	2	3	4	5	6	7	8	9	0
b. Fairness of the test(s)	1	2	3	4	5	6	7	8	9	0
c. Importance of the material on the test(s)	1	2	3	4	5	6	7	8	9	0
d. Wording of questions	1	2	3	4	5	6	7	8	9	0
e. Site monitor's responsiveness during the test(s)	1	2	3	4	5	6	7	8	9	0
f. Instructor's responsiveness after the test(s)	1	2	3	4	5	6	7	8	9	0
g. Score's ability to reflect the knowledge and skills I learned	1	2	3	4	5	6	7	8	9	0

COMMENTS: ____

Course content. Rather than measuring learning assessment of content in this evaluation form, this area provides learner input on the ease of learning the subject matter. Other evaluations or tests can be administered to check on the learner's level of subject matter expertise and understanding of application.

Media. TV is a visual medium, so how did the course come across on the other side of the lens? Were your visuals easy to read, and were the support materials helpful? How closely did support materials align with the live delivery? These are all important questions.

Testing. If you administer tests at the remote site, you'll want to consider including this section in the development of your evaluation tools.

Comments section. It is very important to include this section, which covers areas of importance that you have not listed but are important from an individual perspective.

As with all evaluation tools, you will determine how to collect and analyze information to provide continuous process improvement for your distance learning courses. You will want to include all key stakeholders in discussing and sharing information gained from your evaluation tools and methods.

Lessons Learned in Developing Evaluation Tools

The lessons learned from those who have already delivered courses via distance learning can help provide a foundation of possibilities as you design your own tools and methods. Here are the findings of a Department of Energy study conducted by Denise Macklin and Jeff Hoffman in 1996:

- Traditional classroom evaluation methods can be successfully adapted for use at a distance, particularly for instructional television courses.
- Site facilitators can serve effectively as the eyes, ears and hands of evaluators, as well as instructors at a distance.
- Multiple evaluation methods can be used and validated for each other.
- Collection techniques can include approaches that accommodate several communication styles: verbal, written and behavioral.

In this chapter, we have listed the most common types of questions used to effectively measure success at the remote sites. Now we will focus on ways to provide learner support systems to help the achievement of learning goals.

CHAPTER TWENTY-THREE

Learner Support System Design

INTRODUCTION

At the beginning of the book, we wrote about the new distance learning mindset for trainers. As training professionals, we are not in the center of the training universe, it is the learner that forms the nucleus of the new environment. Yet our role as facilitator, guide, and mentor plays the most important part in the success of distance learning course delivery. Our thinking now goes from "What can I teach?" to "How can I facilitate the learning process for learners?" Being a facilitator of learning requires thinking about those factors that can enhance or detract from both the learning experience and the achievement of successful learning outcomes.

We believe that the new role for trainers holds far more responsibilities than the traditional job description for trainers. There is no longer a traditional job description because distance learning and the constant introduction of new technologies are creating an environment in which we can't think simply in ink. "Tradition" has become a fluid process of delivering training when and where the workforce needs it.

Workers want and need training, education, and information access at home, on the job, and at points in between. To provide 360-degree support, we need to develop and maintain a systematic way of dealing with the need for information, guidance, help, and easy access to additional resources to support the lifelong learning process.

To design effective support systems, it is helpful to look at each step in the distance learning process through the eyes of a learner and to identify what we can do to design learner support systems that facilitate the ease, motivation, and successful outcome at each step along the way.

In this chapter we will identify key result areas for the effective design of learner support systems and services before, during, and after course delivery. Those areas include the following:

- preparation and design of registration processes
- marketing methods and communication vehicles
- learner orientation tools
- self-directed learning resource information.

To effectively design effective support systems, we must first identify the needs of our learners. Let's "see" what thoughts go through the mind of a distance learning learner. What can we do as training professionals to be proactive in addressing these areas? And what would we want and need if we were the learner? As you read these questions, think about the resources you can provide, the information pieces you can create, and the operational processes you can develop.

Here are common thoughts of remote site learners:

- What is distance learning?

- Is it as good as on-site training?
- How does it work?
- Will I have to figure out everything myself?
- What if I don't know how to use the technology?
- How do I register?
- How often will this course be available?
- What if I get sick on the day of the course?
- Where do I send homework assignments or project-related work?
- Will I enjoy this?
- Will it be fun?
- Is someone going to give a lecture on TV?
- Will I have to take a test?
- How will that work?
- How and when will I get my test scores?
- If I have questions about the materials, whom do I ask?
- Who has done this before?
- Where do I buy the books I need (if any) for the course?
- Does the instructor know what I need to use the information for my job? (What will the program do for me?)
- Am I just going to be a number?
- Who else is taking this course?
- Will I get a certificate like the one for learners in the on-site courses?
- Will they know what I am doing if they can't see me?
- What if I have a question that I don't want the world to hear? (How do I ask a personal question?)
- Whom can I call after the course for help?
- What type of help is available?

Whew! These are common, often anxiety-filled questions for new distance learners. We need to prepare our systems to proactively address these areas and allow for continuous input and feedback to ensure that our learners are motivated, and have a sense of security to learn at a distance. As you look at these questions, see where they can be addressed in the following key areas of designing learner support systems.

Preparation and Design of the Registration Process

Looking at your current registration process for on-site courses, can you adapt any process for distance learning registration? The goal is to keep it simple for the learner and easily accessible from any part of the globe. Telephone, fax machine, mail, electronic methods—determine which ones will work best for you and your learners. It would be helpful if you could design your registration form to include a section for capturing key profile information about the learner. This section can include places for job title, skill or knowledge level of this subject, desired learning outcomes, and motivation for taking the course as well as any other data that could help the instructor or support staff target meaningful follow-up and individualized guidance. You could title this section "Getting to Know You" or something similar to help humanize the distance learning experience.

Marketing Methods and Communication Vehicles

It's great that you have selected and designed courses for distance learning delivery. Now you want to get the word out in as many ways as possible. Based on your budget and available resources, you'll want to create marketing pieces that

- have a polished, professional appearance (perhaps with a distance learning logo)
- clearly identify the benefits of taking the course
- explain how to register for the distance learning course
- tell the person whom to call for further information
- include quotes, if possible, from enthusiastic distance learners about the enjoyment and value of this new way of learning
- list upcoming courses or future offerings.

You may decide to have a variety of marketing methods of delivery—using any or all of the ways learners access information about training courses. The most important point here is to use every method possible, not just one. Just as learners each have their own learning style, different people respond differently to various sizes, shapes, colors, and delivery vehicles of marketing media. Where one method may have lukewarm acceptance, another can flood the registration desk with requests! Because people have so many different learning styles, and most we don't know, getting the message out in as many ways as possible will enhance your chances of getting learners to register. Videotape, audio, flyers, brochures, e-mail—you can create the menu of delivery methods to surround your employees with the great news about new course offerings.

Learner Orientation Tools

We discussed remote site materials in an earlier chapter, but it is important to underline the importance of designing tools that are simple to use and easy to understand. The what, where, how, why, and who of the distance learning experience should be detailed in these tools.

Always provide a help line telephone number learners can use in the event they have questions on any aspect of the material. It is comforting for distance learners to know whom to call for what type of question. It might be helpful to box this information up front in the orientation kit.You may have the instructor contact name and information about the hours of availability as well as details on addresses and numbers for mail, phone, fax, and e-mail.

For administrative questions, use the same guidelines. You may have additional resource staff that you want to include in this section of your orientation guide. We never want distance learners to feel that we're leaving them on their own. We want to create a motivational, supportive environment from the very beginning and to encourage learner contact based on their individual needs, in any aspect that can support a successful learning experience.

Self-Directed Learning Resource Information

With the world now at our fingertips via the computer, distance educators can provide focused resource information for every distance learner. An important part of a distance educators' overall support systems is helping learners access self-directed information, whether they want information about a subject content area, related readings, or multimedia resources; financial guidance about taking courses; a menu of related courses; or something else.

The libraries of the world are accessed by a keystroke. Compile a list of computer-based addresses that would be relevant for your course. Perhaps even describe a list server (see Appendix C) that would allow the learners to have a dialogue with others interested in the same type of information. Recommending the list server to learners also encourages them to have a conversation by computer (known as a chat) with others, which expands the networking opportunities to new dimensions! If the learner does not have a computer, most main libraries do, and will provide a wealth of new ideas to enhance the lessons learned during your live session.

This chapter can help you think about the most important areas of learner support. You may uncover others that are unique to your organizational needs and will become part of the foundation of your program. The most important point we want to make is not to forget this area in your strategic planning and budgeting process. Continuous input from learners and your distance learning team members will allow you to modify, enhance, or change learner support systems to meet ever-changing needs and new requirements.

To close this section, we want to share two timeline examples. The first one is for delivering a specific distance learning course. The second one is a master timeline schedule for implementing distance learning within your organization. These examples are included to help guide the creation of your own timelines, based on individual needs or requirements, or both.

We close this section with the knowledge that it is the beginning of your pathway. The road to distance learning has no finish line as the 21st century will create challenges and opportunities not yet identified. You are ready to meet them head on!

Program/Course Implementation Timeline

Program	Activity
3–9 months	Identify instructors; develop budget and marketing plan; identify locations; select dates; reserve rooms, phone lines, equipment; contact site coordinators; develop team and personnel contact list.
2 1/2–8 months	Hold a team planning meeting; plan program design, participant guide, visuals and print materials; implement a marketing plan.
2–6 months	Do first draft of program design, participant guide, visuals and print materials; clear copyright materials.
1–3 months	Do final draft of program design and related materials.
3–9 weeks	Prepare instructor profile; prepare a participant welcome letter and incorporate bio form information; hold on-line practice sessions.
2–6 weeks	Send welcome letter, materials, and *participant guide (see page 126) to site coordinator(s); develop a class roster.
1–3 weeks	Call sites to check on materials, equipment, refreshments, etc.; hold final team meeting; rehearse; contact site coordinator(s) to ensure receipt of materials; implement a technical connection to all sites.
Day of Program	
Early in the day	Review program details and check with team members.
One hour before course	Set up equipment, organize materials, check room set-ups.
15–20 minutes prior to course	Connect sites to bridge.
Scheduled time	Conduct program.
ASAP	Conduct necessary follow-up.

This timeline indicates when to perform what activity during planning of a distance learning course.

Program Timeline developed by Rosemary Lehman, UW-Extension, 1995, appears in Lehman, Rosemary (1996). *The Essential Compressed Video Guide: 7 Keys to Success*, Instructional Communications Systems, UW-Extension: Madison, WI (p. 10). Permission to reprint this copyrighted material is given by Instructional Communications Systems.

Sample Distance Learning Implementation Master Timeline - The First 12 Months

We are often asked by organizations, "What should I be doing now?" Of course the answer to that depends on where your organization is on its distance learning journey. The timeline below is provided as a sample of how you might phase the various tasks associated with implementing distance learning.

Look at the columns labeled "Month 1, Month 2, Month 3…". Then read down and you will get a feel for what activities should be going on during that time frame. For example, during the first 90 days (Months 1-3) you should "assess the need" for distance learning. You should also "form your distance learning team" and have some members of the team "experience it as a student." As you look at the bottom of the chart, you see that you should attend trade shows, conferences, and vendor demonstrations at the onset and throughout your entire distance learning journey.

We realize that some events may be dependent on your getting additional resources. For example, you may be able to begin training instructors using existing resources, or that step may not be able to be accomplished until you get additional funding. You will develop your own timeline based on your organization's particular situation.

<table>
<tr><th>Month 1</th><th>Month 2</th><th>Month 3</th><th>Month 4</th><th>Month 5</th><th>Month 6</th><th>Month 7</th><th>Month 8</th><th>Month 9</th><th>Month 10</th><th>Month 11</th><th>Month 12</th></tr>
<tr><td colspan="3">Assess the need.</td><td colspan="4">Prepare distance learning strategic plan.</td><td colspan="5"></td></tr>
<tr><td colspan="2">Form your distance learning team.</td><td colspan="4">Prepare cost-benefit analysis.</td><td colspan="3">Program for funding. Integrate with your budget cycle.</td><td colspan="3">Obtain funding. Integrate with your budget cycle.</td></tr>
<tr><td colspan="3">Experience it! as a student.</td><td colspan="6">Experience it! manage and conduct a pilot distance learning event.</td><td colspan="3"></td></tr>
<tr><td colspan="3"></td><td colspan="9">Train instructors, instructional designers, remote site coordinators, and support personnel. Use pilot events to start the process. Institutionalize and provide continuous improvement.</td></tr>
<tr><td colspan="4"></td><td colspan="8">Begin transitioning courses. Use pilot events to start the process. Institutionalize and provide continuous improvement.</td></tr>
<tr><td colspan="4"></td><td colspan="8">Develop a standardized participant packet. Use pilot events to start the process. Institutionalize and provide continuous improvement.</td></tr>
<tr><td colspan="5"></td><td colspan="7">Design and implement learner support systems. Use pilot events to start the process. Institutionalize and provide continuous improvement.</td></tr>
<tr><td colspan="3"></td><td colspan="3">Evaluate and select technologies based on learners' needs.</td><td colspan="6"></td></tr>
<tr><td colspan="5"></td><td colspan="3">Develop installation plan for distance learning equipment.</td><td colspan="4">Install and deliver distance learning equipment.</td></tr>
<tr><td colspan="12">Attend trade shows, conferences and vendor demonstrations.</td></tr>
<tr><td colspan="12">Visit organizations using distance learning (benchmarking).</td></tr>
</table>

The master timeline shows when to perform tasks during implementation of distance learning in an organization.

At training conferences and at client meetings, people often ask us, "Where can we go to get the information we need as trainers?"

When we started on our journey, it was a time-consuming process to find out, and we didn't know what we didn't know. We initially left out important steps that proved to be costly and time-consuming, and we did not include others because we were not aware of their importance. We didn't know what we didn't know! And we were not convinced that distance learning would really work.

Now, we look back and feel gratified by seeing how well our learners succeed at accomplishing learning objectives and effectively applying the lessons learned with different types of distance learning delivery options. And they are enthusiastic about learning with a hybrid approach to course delivery. What a sense of accomplishment for a trainer!

In a recent article on innovations in technology, the focus was on how your TV is currently being converged with a PC. There are currently over 40 million people in the United States alone who have chosen not to have a PC at home. Multiply that by the percentage of the world population that does not have a PC, but does have a television. Web TV will allow you to have interactive television right in your home. Imagine this: Plan your vacation with your family and select different options to "visit" your destination before making your decision. Like football? You can watch the game and instantly be able to access player statistics on the Internet at the same time. From a training perspective, just think about the possibilities of offering interactive training courses through a home television. The new integration methods and ideas that technology offers provide not only a means to achieving bottom-line goals in your organization but also a way for people to continue lifelong learning development in their homes.

The future is exciting and filled with options. Think about what you can do with the talent you have right now. To teach is to touch a life forever. Distance learning will allow you to reach many people and teach them what they need to know in order to become skilled 21st-century professionals. You are in a pivotal position to make it happen.

Best wishes for your success.

The following glossary will be helpful as you encounter new terms in doing research or in speaking with others about distance learning.

Analog—Information that is transmitted by means of modulations of a continuous signal, such is a radio wave; see Digital.

Audiographics—The transmission of images and graphics over ordinary telephone lines to enhance audio interaction. The audiographics family includes electronic whiteboards, electronic tablets, computers, still video systems, computer-based multimedia systems or combinations thereof.

Audio teleconferencing—Two-way voice communication between two or more groups, or three or more individuals, who are in separate locations linked by a telecommunications medium.

Audiotext—An automated computer-based telephone messaging technology, it operates similar to an answering machine. It allows for calling a computer and tapping into information on a 24 hour basis.

Bandwidth—The range of frequencies that can be carried by a telecommunications medium without undue distortion, such as a broadcast television signal of 3 million Hertz or a telephone voice signal of 3,000 Hertz.

Bit—Binary digit, the smallest unit of information in a computer.

Bridge—A device that is designed to interconnect three or more telephone lines; used to link multiple locations for audio or audiographic teleconferencing.

Broadband—A telecommunications medium that carries high frequency signals; includes television frequencies of 3 to 6 million Hertz.

Broadcast—The one-way transmission of information.

Byte—The unit of computer memory typically consisting of 8 bits; 64K 64,000 bytes or 64 kilobytes.

C-Band—The range of frequencies from 4-6 gigahertz on which most satellites and terrestrial microwave systems receive and transmit signals.

Cable TV—Transmits programs to subscribers through coaxial cable rather than over the air. Most cable systems have the potential for two-way communication in addition to broadcast television.

CAD—Computer Aided Design.

CCTV—(Closed-Circuit-Television), the system for sending cable signals to subscribers or designated locations.

CD-I—Computer Disc Interactive.

CD-V—Computer Disc Video.

CD-ROM—Computer Disc, Read Only Memory.

Compressed Video—Video images that have been compressed to remove redundant information, thereby reducing the amount of bandwidth required to send them over a telecommunications channel.

Computer Conferencing—Allows individuals at different locations to communicate with each other through computers.

Digital—Electronic information based on the binary code, sent as a series of on/off pulses and is less subject to interference.

DBS—(Direct Broadcast Satellite) a satellite designed with sufficient power that smaller earth stations can be used for direct on-site reception of signals.

Downlink—(Verb) the process of beaming signals from a satellite to earth stations; (noun) an antenna shaped like a dish that receives signals from a satellite.

Downstream—An audio or video signal traveling from the cable TV headend to a subscriber point in the community.

Electronic Banking—Financial transactions via videotex or on-line computer.

Electronic Whiteboard or Blackboard—A device that looks like an ordinary whiteboard or blackboard but has a special conductive surface for creating freehand information that can be send over a telecommunications channel, usually a telephone line.

Electronic Bulletin Board—Holds information that can be accessed by computers via a modem.

E-Mail—(Electronic-Mail), messages sent to and from a computer or videotex terminal linked by telephone lines.

Fax or Facsimile—Copies of documents and graphics that are sent via phone lines to another copier.

Fiber Optics—A technology that transmits voice, video and data by sending digital pulses of light through hair-thin strands of flexible glass.

Footprint—The geographic area on the globe in which a given satellite signal can be received.

Geosynchronous Orbit—The altitude 22,300 miles above the equator at which the satellite's orbit is synchronous with the earth's rotation, making the satellite appear stationary.

GigaHertz—One billion Hertz (cycles per second).

Hardware—A term used for electronic equipment.

HDTV—(High Definition Television), doubles the number of lines in a broadcast or cablecast signal, creating a very high resolution signal.

Headend—A cable system's central location, where it receives, amplifies, and converts incoming signals before redistributing them to subscribers.

Interactive Technology—Technology that permits two-way participation.

Interface—The place at which two systems or pieces of equipment meet and interact with each other.

ISDN—(Integrated Services Digital Network), a digital telecommunications channel that allows for the integrated transmission of voice, video and data.

ITFS—(Instructional Television Fixed Service), a group of channels in the ultra high frequency range that has been set aside since the 1960s for educational use. It transmits via microwave equipment not more than 20-30 miles (line of sight) from the transmitter.

Ka-Band—A satellite transmission in the 20 and 30 gigahertz frequency spectrum; still an experimental technology.

KiloHertz—One thousand Hertz cycles per second).

Kilo-Band—A satellite transmission in the 11 to 14 gigahertz frequency spectrum; a newer technology than C-Band.

Ku-band—A satellite transmission in the 12 and 14 gigahertz frequency spectrum.

Laser—Light amplification by stimulated emission of radiation. This highly focused beam of light (or its device) is used in fiber optics and optical video disc.

LPTV—(Low Power Television), a weak signal that can be squeezed between existing channels, without causing interference. It has been authorized by the FCC for broadcast to small geographic areas.

MDS—Pay television delivery service relayed by microwave to small dish antennas.

Meet-Me-Bridge—A type of telephone bridge that can be accessed directly by calling a certain telephone number; provides dial-in teleconferencing.

MegaHertz—One million Hertz (cycles per second).

Microprocessor—The heart of the computer. A silicon chip that processes data and controls the computer's components.

Microwave—High frequency radio waves, above 500 megahertz , that can transmit television signals. They are easily disturbed by trees, buildings, etc., and require direct line-of-site to operate.

Modem—(Modulation-Demodulation), the hardware that facilitates communication between two or more computers.

Multiplexor—Equipment used to combine signals from different sources for transmission over a single channel.

Narrowband—A telecommunications medium that carries low frequency signals, such as telephone voice signals.

Narrowcast—Sending out television or audio signals to a small, narrow, specific audience.

On-Line—In direct communication with a computer.

Optical Video Disc—(Laser Disc), a video playback laser beam is reflected against microscopic pits on a disc to retrieve frames of prerecorded information. The disc can contain more than 54,000 frames that can be located instantly.

Random Access—Locating information at any point on a disc.

Room Integration—Design or construction of a total teleconferencing room, including the equipment, associated electronics, and environment.

Satellite—An orbiting antenna, also called a "bird," that relays signals (voice, data and video) from and back to earth.

Software—Programs created for computer use.

SCA—(Subsidiary Communication Authorization), radio version of vertical blanking intervals (VBI). Public institutions that have access to FM have access to SCA.

Telecommunications—The use of wire, radio, optical or other electromagnetic channel to transmit or receive signals for voice, video and data communications; communications over distance using electrical means.

Teleconferencing—Two-way electronic communication between two or more groups, or three or more individuals, who are in separate locations; includes group communication via audio, audiographics, video and computer systems.

Teleport—a facility, usually in large urban areas, that offers various telecommunications services.

Teletext—One-way textual graphic information sent on unused scanning lines.

Transponder—The device on a satellite that receives, amplifies and retransmits audio, video and data signals from the earth.

TVRO—(Television Receive Only), consists of an antenna (dish), low-noise block downconverter and a satellite receiver. The antenna size varies with location.

UHF—(Ultra High Frequency), channels 14-69.

Upstream—An audio or video signal traveling from a subscriber point in the cabled community to the cable TV headend.

VBI—(Vertical Blanking Interval), the 21 unused lines on television that appear as a heavy black line when the horizontal hold slops. These lines are useful for messages for the blind, E-Mail and other data.

VHF—(Very High Frequency), channels 1-13.

VHS—(Video Home System), the most common type of video home recorder. The less common system is called Beta. They are not compatible.

Video Teleconferencing—Two-way voice and video between two or more groups, or three or more individuals, who are in separate locations linked by a telecommunications medium.

Videotex—An interactive technology that uses phone line or two-way cable to connect the television set to a central computer. The user retrieves information or transacts business using a keypad or keyboard.

Videotext—Identical to audiotext, with the exception that it utilizes video.

Viewdata—Identical to videotex.

Virtual Space—A type of video conference in which each participant is assigned to separate camera and is seen on a separate monitor, large screen or assigned spatial area.

Reprinted from *Distance Education Technology,* Core Module, Distance Education Professional Development Program, University of Wisconsin-Madison, pp. 120-123.

Distance Learning Equipment and Service Vendors

The following list is not meant to be all inclusive. New businesses and service providers enter the marketplace as rapidly as new opportunities arise from technological advances. However, we wanted to provide a starting point for our readers as they begin to gather vendor information on various distance learning products and services. We hope this list will save you time and prove helpful as you begin to build your own list.

Audio Conferencing Equipment

A.T. Products, Inc.
1600 S. Division Street
Harvard, IL 60033
Phone: 815/943-3590
Fax: 815/943-3604

Polycom, Inc.
2584 Junction Avenue
San Jose, CA 95134-1902
Phone: 800/POLYCOM
Fax: 408/526-9100
http://www.ite.net/polycom.htm

Shure Brothers, Inc.
222 Hartley Avenue
Evanston, IL 60202
Phone: 847/866-2200
Fax: 847/866-2279

TelAid Industries, Inc.
1 World Trade Center, Suite 8955
New York, NY 10048
Phone: 815/334-8835
Fax: 815/334-8836

U.S. Robotics
7770 N. Frontage Road
Skokie, IL 60077
Phone: 800/342-5877
Fax: 847/676-7320
http://www.usrobotics.com

Audio Conference Service Providers

AT&T Executive Teleconferencing
420 3rd Avenue South, Room 901
Minneapolis, MN 55415
Phone: 800/932-1100
Fax: 800/742-6895

ConferTech International
12110 N. Pecos Street
Westminster, CO 80234
Phone: 303/633-3413
Fax: 303/633-3409

networkMCI Conferencing
8750 W. Bryn Mawr #900
Chicago, IL 60631
Phone: 312/399-4439
Fax: 312/399-1716

Sprint Meeting Channel
3065 Cumberland Circle
Atlanta, GA 30339
Phone: 404/649-1225
Fax: 404/649-1240

Audiographic Conferencing Equipment

Live Works
Xerox Corporation
5230 Pacific Concourse Drive
Suite 200, Office 235
Los Angeles, CA 90045
Phone: 800/200-1167
Fax: 310/649-4499
http://www.liveworks.com

Optel Communications
50 Jackson Avenue
Syosset, NY 11791
Phone: 516/921-3700
Fax: 516/921-3709

Instructor Training

AT&T Center for Excellence in
Distance Learning
15 W. 6th Street, Room 729
Cincinnati, OH 45202
Phone: 800/590-CEDL (2335)
Fax: 513/352-7923

Distance Learning Integrators, Inc.
4707 Lehigh Court
Dale City, VA 22193
Phone: 703/590-0430
Fax: 703/590-0506
dlii@aol.com

Quiet Power, Inc.
1201 Pennsylvania Avenue
Suite 300
Washington, DC 20004
Phone: 202/661-4646
Fax: 202/661-4699
QuietPower@aol.com

Teletraining Institute
370 Student Union
Oklahoma State University
Stillwater, OK 74078-0801
Phone: 405/744-7510
Fax: 405/744-7511

Xerox Document University
P.O. Box 2000 Route 7659
Leesburg, VA 22075
Phone: 705/729-8000

Interactive Television Equipment

AT&T Tridom
840 Franklin Court
Marietta, GA 30067
Phone: 404/514-3727
Fax: 404/514-1737

COMSAT/RSI
6560 Rock Spring Drive
Bethesda, MD 20817
Phone: 703/450-5680
Fax: 703/450-4894

Hughes Communications
GM Hughes Electronics
P.O. Box 92424
Los Angeles, CA 90009
Phone: 310/607-4193
Fax: 310/607-4065

Miralite Communications
4040 MacArthur Boulevard, #307
Newport Beach, CA 92660
Phone: 714/474-1900
Fax: 714/474-1885

Internet/Intranet Web Authoring and Browser Software

Corel WordPerfect
Corel Corporation
1600 Carling Avenue
Ottawa, Ontario, Canada K1Z 8R7
Phone: 613/728-3733
Fax: 613/761-9176

Microsoft Front Page /Microsoft Internet Explorer
Microsoft Corporation
1 Microsoft Way
Redmond, WA 98052-8300
Phone: 206/882-8080
http://www.microsoft.com

Netscape Navigator
Netscape Communications Corporation
501 E. Middlefield Road
Mountain View, CA 94043-4042
Phone: 415/254-1900
http://www.netscape.com

Mapping Software

MapInfo Software
One Global View
Troy, NY 12180-8399
Phone: 800/552-2511
Fax: 518/285-7575

Multimedia Authoring Software

Authorware
Macromedia Corporation
San Francisco, CA
Phone: 800/756-9603
Fax: 415/626-0554
http://www.macromedia.com

IconAuthor
AimTech Corporation
Nashua, NH
Phone: 800/289-2884
Fax: 603/883-5582
http://www.aimtech.com

Macromedia Director
Macromedia Corporation
San Francisco, CA
Phone: 800/756-9603
Fax: 415/626-0554
http://www.macromedia.com

Multimedia Toolbook
Asymetrix Corporation
Bellevue, WA
Phone: 800/448-6543
Fax: 206/455-3071
http://www.asymetrix.com

Multimedia Personal Computers

Compaq Computer Corporation
20555 Sh 249
Houston, TX 77070
Phone: 800/345-1518
http://www.compaq.com

Dell Computer Corporation
2214 W. Braker Lane, Suite D
Austin, TX 78758
Phone: 800/424-1370
http://www.dell.com

Gateway 2000
610 Gateway Drive
Sioux City, SD 57049-2000
Phone: 888/888-0242
Fax: 605/232-2023
http://www.gw2k.com

Hewlett-Packard Co.
Cupertino, CA
Phone: 800/724-6631
Fax: 800/357-1317
http://www.hp.com

IBM
IBM Consumer Division
Research Triangle Park, NC
Phone: 800/426-7235
Fax: 800/426-4329
http://www.pc.ibm.com

Unisys Corporation
Township Line & Union Meeting Roads
Blue Bell, PA 19424-0001
Phone 800-874-8647, ext. 582
Outside US and Canada 716/742-6780
http://www.unisys.com

Program and Systems Integration

Convergent Media Systems Corporation
3490 Piedmont Road
Atlanta, GA 30305
Phone: 404/262-1555
Fax: 404/262-2055

CritiCom, Inc.
4211 Forbes Blvd.
Lanham, MD 20706
Phone: 301/306-0600
Fax: 301/306-0605

Distance Learning Integrators, Inc.
4707 Lehigh Court
Dale City, VA 22193
Phone: 703/590-0430
Fax: 703/590-0506
dlii@aol.com

Pierce-Phelps, Inc.
2000 N. 59th Street
Philadelphia, PA 19131-3099
Phone: 215/879-7131
Fax: 215/878-5252

Quiet Power, Inc.
1201 Pennsylvania Avenue
Suite 300
Washington, DC 20004
Phone: 202/661-4646
Fax: 202/661-4699
QuietPower@aol.com

Satellite Network Service Providers

Unisys Television Services
Steve Fanelli, Director
Township Line and Union Meeting Roads
Blue Bell, PA 19424
Phone: 215/986-3809
Fax: 215/986-2626

Westcott Communications, Inc.
1303 Marsh Lane
Carrolton, TX 75006
Phone: 214/417-4100
Fax: 214/716-5109

Satellite Program Providers

AMA by Satellite
American Management Association
135 W. 50th Street
New York, NY 10020-1201
Phone: 212/903-8115
Fax: 212/903-8329

PBS Adult Learning Service
Attention: Shirley Davis
1320 Braddock Place
Alexandria, VA 22314
Phone: 703/739-5146
Fax: 703/739-8495
E-mail: sdavis@pbs.org

U.S. Chamber of Commerce
Kandace Laass
1615 H. Street NW
Washington, DC 20062
Phone: 202/463-5431
Fax: 202/463-5651

Video Teleconferencing Equipment

Compression Labs, Inc. (CLI)
2860 Junction Avenue
San Jose, CA 95120
Phone: 408/435-3000
Fax: 408/922-5429

PictureTel
222 Rosewood Drive
Danvers, MA 01923
Phone: 508/762-5435
Fax: 508/762-5239

VTEL
108 Wild Basin Road
Austin, TX 78746
Phone: 512/314-2755
Fax: 512/314-2792

Video Teleconferencing Networks for Lease

Kinkos Videoconferencing Rooms
(Partnership with Sprint)
Phone: 800/669-1235.
http://www.kinkos.com/products/catalog/video

Sprint Video
3065 Cumberland Circle
Atlanta, GA 30339
Phone: 800/669-1235
Fax: 404/989-1362

Viewer Response Pads

Audience Response Systems Inc.
2148 N. Cullen Avenue
Evansville, IN 47715
Phone: 800/468-6583
Fax: 812/479-1057

One Touch Systems, Inc.
3295 Scott Blvd., Suite 200
Santa Clara, CA 95054
Phone: 408/727-3933
Fax: 408/727-1848

Organizations Using Distance Learning

You can help kick start your initiative by visiting and benchmarking with organizations that have already institutionalized distance learning as a means of training their workforce or customers. The following list is a fraction of the organizations in both the private and public sectors that have ongoing distance learning initiatives. You may use it to begin networking with other organizations. We have found that most of those who have successful programs are willing to showcase their networks to others.

Corporations

CompUSA
14951 Dallas Parkway 10th
Dallas, TX 75240-7570
Phone: 214/383-4000
http://www.compusa.com

Ford Motor Company
FordStar
330 Town Center Drive
Fairlane Plaza South
Suite 324
Dearborn, MI 48126

Hewlett-Packard Company
19483 Pruneridge Avenue, MS48NL
Cupertino, CA 95014
Phone: 800/724-6631
Fax: 800/357-1317
http://www.hp.com

Home Depot
2727 Paces Ferry Road NW
Atlanta, GA 30339-4089
Phone: 770/433-8211

Management Recruiters International, Inc.
200 Public Square, 31st Floor
Cleveland, OH 44114-2301
Phone: 216/696-1122
Fax: 216/696-3221

Microsoft TV
Microsoft Corporation
1 Microsoft Way
Redmond, WA 98052-8300
Phone: 206/882-8080
http://www.microsoft.com

Oracle Corporation
500 Oracle Parkway
Redwood Shores, CA 94065
Phone: 415/506-7000

Unisys
Unisys Television Services
Steve Fanelli, Director
Township Line & Union Meeting Roads
Blue Bell, PA 19424
Phone: 215/986-3809
Fax: 215/986-2626

Associations

American Society for Training and Development
1640 King Street
Box 1443
Alexandria, VA 22313-2043
Phone: 703/683-8100
Fax: 703/683-8103

Federal Governmental Agencies

Department of Energy
Central Training Academy
P.O. Box 5400
Albuquerque, NM 87117
Phone: 505/845-4808
Fax: 505/845-6079

Environmental Protection Agency
Mail Code: 2235A
401 M Street SW
Washington, DC 20460
Phone: 202/564-2632
Fax: 202/564-0075

Federal Aviation Administration
DOT/FAA/Academy/AMA-300B2
Training Support Division
P.O. Box 25082
Oklahoma City, OK 73065
Phone: 405/9546913
Fax: 405/954-9507

Internal Revenue Service
U.S. Department of the Treasury
IVT Distance Learning Team Leader
221 S. Clark Street
Crystal Plaza 6, Suite 212
Arlington, VA 22202-3799
Phone: 703/308-6068
Fax: 703/308-6543

Social Security Administration
U.S. Department of Health and Human Services
6401 Security Boulevard
Room 4400
Woodlawn, MD 21235
Phone: 410/965-1961
Fax: 410/965-2496

U.S. Air Force
HQ Air University/HQ AU/XOL
55 LeMay Plaza South
Maxwell AFB, AL 36112-6335
Phone: 334/953-7026
Fax: 334/953-4148

U.S. Air National Guard
ANG/SCTT
3500 Fetchet Avenue
Andrews AFB, MD 20762-5157
Phone: 301/836-8631
Fax: 301/836-8761

U.S. Army
Satellite Education Network (SEN)
Building 12500
2401 Quarters Road
Ft. Lee, VA 23801-1705
Phone: 804/765-4004
Fax: 804/765-4663

U.S. Army National Guard
Attn: NGB-ARO-TS
111 South George Mason Drive
Arlington, VA 22204-1382
Phone: 703/607-9317
Fax: 703/607-7385

Veterans Benefits Administration
Office of Employee Development Training
1000 Legion Place, Suite 1520
Orlando, FL 32801
Phone: 407/648-6161
Fax: 407/648-6163

Academic Institutions

Academic institutions have long used various forms of distance learning to increase their outreach. You may be surprised to discover a wealth of information on distance learning at the university or community college in your own backyard.

Arizona State University
Tempe, AZ 85287
Phone: 602/965-9011

Indiana Higher Education Training System
957 W. Michigan Street
Indianapolis, IN 46202
Phone: 317/263-8900
Fax: 317/263-8831

Iowa State University
Extended and Continuing Education
Ames, IA 50011-1120
515/294-6222

Kentucky Educational Television (KET)
600 Cooper Drive
Lexington, KY 40502
Phone: 606/258-7254
Fax: 606/258-7390

Old Dominion University
TELETECHNET
Norfolk, VA 23529
Phone: 800/968-2638
Fax: 757/683-5492

Oklahoma State University
Stillwater, OK 74078
Phone: 405/744-5000

Pennsylvania State University
403 South Allen Street, Suite 206
University Park, PA 16801-5202
Phone: 814/863-3764

Utah State University
Logan, UT 84322
Phone: 801/750-1000

University of Wisconsin-Madison
Attention: Dr. Christine Olgren
225 North Mills Street, Room 112
Madison, WI 53706
Phone: 608/262-8530
Fax: 608/262-7751
E-mail: cholgren@macc.wisc.edu

University of Maryland
University Blvd. at Adelphi Road
College Park, MD 20742

Distance Learning Reference Materials

Where do I get more information? How do I stay current on distance learning issues? What are some good distance learning resources on the Internet? Those are some of the questions you might have as you continue your distance learning past implementation and onto continuous improvement. The following list will help point you in the right direction toward building an organizational library of distance learning resources for your distance learning team.

Books

Duning, Becky, Marvin Van Kekerix, and Leon Zaborowski. *Reaching Learners Through Telecommunications.* San Francisco: Jossey-Bass, 1993.

Krebs, Arlene. *The Distance Learning Funding Sourcebook.* Kendall/Hunt Publishing Company, 1996.

Lochte, R.H. Interactive *Television and Instruction: A Guide to Technology, Technique, Facilities Design, and Classroom Management.* Englewood Cliffs, NJ: Educational Technology Publications, 1993.

Piskurich, George. *The ASTD Handbook of Instructional Technology.* New York: McGraw-Hill/ASTD, 1993.

Portway, Patrick, and Carla Lane. 2d Edition. *Guide to Teleconferencing & Distance Learning.* San Ramon, CA: Applied teleCommunications, 1994.

Rowntree, Derek. *Exploring Open and Distance Learning.* London, United Kingdom: Kogan Page Limited, 1992.

Wagner, Ellen. *Variables Affecting Distance Educational Program Success.* Englewood Cliffs, NJ: Educational Technology Publications, 1993.

Willis, Barry. *Distance Education: A Practical Guide.* Englewood Cliffs, NJ: Educational Technology Publications, 1993.

Willis, Barry. *Distance Education Strategies and Tools.* Englewood Cliffs, NJ: Educational Technology Publications, 1993.

Periodicals

The American Journal of Distance Education
The Pennsylvania State University
110 Rackley Building
University Park, PA 16802-3202
Phone: 814/863-3764
Fax: 814/865-5878

ED—Education at a Distance
Applied Business teleCommunications
Box 5106
San Ramon, CA 94583
Phone: 510/606-5150
Fax: 510/606-9410

Teleconference
Applied Business teleCommunications
Box 5106
San Ramon, CA 94583
Phone: 510/606-5150
Fax: 510/606-9410

Teleconferencing Business
Teleconferencing Business, Inc.
18 Hudson Road
Garden City, NY 11530
Phone: 516/775-4247
Fax: 516/775-0849

Distance Learning Associations and Centers

American Center for the Study of Distance Education
Pennsylvania State University
403 South Allen Street, Suite 206
University Park, PA 16801-5202
Phone: 814/863-3764

Distance Education and Training Council
1601 18th Street NW
Washington, DC 20009
Phone: 202/234-5100

Distance Learning Resource Network
WestEd
730 Harrison Street
San Francisco, CA 94107
Phone: 800/662-4160

ITCA
International Teleconferencing Association
1650 Tysons Boulevard, Suite 200
McLean, VA 22102
Phone: 703/506-3280
Fax: 703/506-3266

USDLA
United States Distance Learning Association
P.O. Box 5129
San Ramon, CA 94583
Phone: 510/606-5160
Fax: 510/606-9410

World Wide Web Sites

The list of Web sites dealing with distance learning changes daily. Use your Web browser search function or go to an index site such as Yahoo (http://www.yahoo.com) and search "distance learning," "distance education," and "instructional technology." We have provided a sampling of some of the sites we have found especially useful for getting distance learning information.

Arizona State University Distance Learning Technology
http://www-distlearn.pp.asu.edu/

AT&T Center for Excellence in Distance Learning (CEDL)
http://www.att.com/cedl/

Federal Government Distance Learning Association
http://www.fgdla.org

U.S. Department of Education
http://www.ed.gov/

United States Distance Learning Association
http://www.usdla.org/

University of Maryland System Institute for Distance Education
http://www.umuc.edu/ide/ide.html

University of South Carolina Distance Education and Instructional Support
http://www.sc.edu/deis/

University of Wisconsin Distance Education Clearinghouse
http://www. uwex.edu/disted/home. html

List Servers (Internet Mailing Lists)

Internet list servers provide a way for individuals to communicate and keep informed on various topics. Think of it as a continuous discussion group where all who have "subscribed" to the group may e-mail discussion comments or information to the entire group. To "subscribe," you send an e-mail to the list server address containing the following in the message portion:

SUBSCRIBE listname firstname lastname

EXAMPLE: SUBSCRIBE DEOS-L John Smith

Be advised that depending on how active the discussion group or list server is, you may receive a "generous" amount of e-mail every day. When you subscribe, you will receive instructions on how to "unsubscribe" for that list server. Keep these instructions! You may need them to stop the flow of e-mail if it becomes unmanageable.

We have included one of the more popular distance learning list servers below:

DEOS-L - The Distance Education Online Symposium
List Server Address:
DEOS@PSUVM.PSU.EDU

Distance Learning Professional Certification and Degree Programs

University of Wisconsin-Madison
Attention: Dr. Christine Olgren
225 North Mills Street, Room 112
Madison, WI 53706
Phone: 608/262-8530
Fax: 608/262-7751
E-mail: cholgren@macc.wisc.edu

Trade Shows and Conferences

International Distance Learning Conference (IDLCON)
Applied Business teleCommunications
P.O. Box 5106
San Ramon, CA 94583
Phone: 510/606-5150
Fax: 510/606-9410

ITCA Conference

International Teleconferencing Association
1650 Tysons Boulevard, Suite 200
McLean, VA 22102
Phone: 703/506-3280
Fax: 703/506-3266

Annual Conference on Distance Teaching and Learning
University of Wisconsin-Madison
225 North Mills Street, Room 112
Madison, WI 53706
Phone: 608/262-8530
Fax: 608/262-7751

TeleCon

Applied Business teleCommunications
P.O. Box 5106
San Ramon, CA 94583
Phone: 510/606-5150
Fax: 510/606-9410

DISTANCE LEARNING LITERATURE SEARCH SERVICES

American Society for Training and Development
Information Center
1640 King Street
Box 1443
Alexandria, VA 22313-2043
Phone: 703/683-8184
Fax: 703/683-8103

For more information, ASTD members may call the ASTD Information Center to request a free, customized literature search on distance learning. Members may also access the Member Information Exchange, which provides a customized list of five names and phone numbers of national ASTD members who can provide advice on distance learning. Nonmembers may call the Information Center to obtain the current cost of nonmember literature searches. The Information Center has also compiled a resource guide on distance learning, consisting of full-text articles and a bibliography. Call the Information Center for current pricing on the resource guide.

Chute, A., *The American Journal of Distance Education,* volume 8, number 1, 1994.

Davis, James L., and Thomas W. Smith. "Computer-Assisted Distance Learning, Part I: Audiographic Teleconferencing, Interactive Satellite Broadcasts, and Technical Japanese Instruction from the University of Wisconsin-Madison," IEEE, 1994.

Davis, James L. "Computer-Assisted Distance Learning, Part II: Examination Performance of Students On and Off Campus." Journal of Engineering Education, January 1996.

Defense Technical Information Center: Potential Benefits of Using Video Teleconferencing at AFLC/HQ to Conduct Training, 1988.

Feasley, C., and C. Olgren. *Evaluation for Distance Education.* The Board of Regents of the University of Wisconsin, 1994 (pp. 14-15).

Gooler, D.D. "Evaluating Distance Education Programs," *Canadian Journal of University Continuing Education,* volume 6, number 1, 1979 (pp. 43-55).

Hillman, D., D. Willis, and C.N. Gunawardena. "Learner-Interface Interaction in Distance Education: An Extension of Contemporary Models and Strategies for Practitioners." *The American Journal of Distance Education,* volume 8, number 2, 1994 (pp. 30-42).

Kirkpatrick, D.L. *A Practical Guide for Supervisory Training and Development* (2d edition). Menlo Park, CA: Addison-Wesley, 1983.

Kovacs, Bob. "Advancing Technology: A Corporate Experience," *Technical Communications,* second quarter, 1994.

Lane, G. Kevin. Distance Learning White Paper, AT&T, (February, 1996).

Macklin, D., and J. Hoffman. "Four Learner Interactions That Make the Difference in the Design and Development of Instructional Television (ITV) Courses." Paper presented at 12th Annual Conference on Distance Teaching and Learning, University of Wisconsin-Madison, August 1996.

Mantyla, K. Effective Video Teleconferences Briefings and Meetings, 1996. Washington, DC.

Moore, M.G. "Three Types of Interaction." *The American Journal of Distance Education,* volume 3, number 2, 1989 (pp. 1-6).

Muldoon, Kathleen. "Turning It Won't...Into It Will...And It Does." A Distance Learning Case Study Paper presented at the ASTD Annual Conference June, 1996. Orlando, FL.

Ostendorf, Virginia A. Distance Education Technology, core module, Distance Education Professional Development Program, University of Wisconsin-Madison.

Payne, H., and R. Smith. "Governmental Agencies Turn to Distance Learning for Training." *Teleconference,* volume 14, number 2, (pp. 29-35).

Pennsylvania State University. The Report of the Task Force on Distance Education, November 1992.

PictureTel Learning Cost-Benefit Analysis, PictureTel Corporate Training.

Portway, Patrick S., and Carla Lane. *Technical Guide to Teleconferencing and Distance Learning,* San Ramon, CA. Applied Business teleCommunications, 1992.

Rovinsky, Robert. "Making Investment Decisions: Estimating the Return on Investment." GLTC , April 1996.

Seidel, Robert, and Paul Chatelier. *Learning Without Boundaries: Technology to Support Distance/Distributed Learning,* Plenum Press, 1994.

The Center for Adult Learning and Education Credentials, American Council on Education. "Guiding Principles for Distance Learning in a Learning Society," July 1996.

Thompson, F., S. Larkin, and A. Shogren. "IRS Interactive Training Project." Paper presented to the Government Learning Technology Symposium, April 29-30, 1996; Washington, DC. Proceedings Document (pp. 28-31).

U.S. Congress, Office of Technology Assessment. *Linking for Learning: A New Course for Education,* OTA-SET-430, Washington, DC: U.S. Government Printing Office, November 1989.

Wagner, Ellen. "Instructional Design and Development: Contingency Management for Distance Education." Paper presented to The American Symposium on Research in Distance Education, July 24-27, 1988 (p. 12).

Yoakum, Michael, and Alan G. Chute. *Distance Learning: An Introduction. AT&T Center for Excellence in Distance Learning and Indiana University Center for Excellence in Education,* 1994 (p. 2).

Index

A

B

C

D

Karen dedicates this book to...

my son Mike, who introduced me to the world of computers and technology 13 years ago and who patiently answered my question, "How does this work again?" in a supportive and continuous fashion. When he went off to college, he said, "Now, Mom, you're going to have to start doing this yourself." I did. Thank you, Mike. You constantly inspire me to keep doing my best.

my mother, Sylvia Fischer, who believes that I can do anything in this world. Her belief in my abilities, her positive attitude toward life, and her love helped me to turn my vision of writing this book into reality. My father, Milton Fischer, who provided role-model examples of learning how to do anything and the joy of helping other people.

my wonderful distance learning clients, especially Chaletta McCoy, who had a vision and started with a white sheet of paper to design the best 21st-century distance learning system. Her entrepreneurial thinking, creative ideas, no-nonsense approach to making it happen, and customer-focused initiatives at every step are already turning the vision into real-world success.

and, to my coauthor, Rick, who worked with me (an ENTJ) in a collaborative fashion. We wrote many sections at a distance and used the Internet to attach files and edit along the way. Thanks, Rick, for the synergy, understanding, expertise, commitment, humor, and love you brought to the table in order to turn a vision into our book.

Rick dedicates this book to...

my father, George M. Gividen Jr., a decorated war hero, who taught me by example that one person can make a difference and to always have the courage to "tell it like it is."

Zeke Osburn, U.S. Postal Service Technical Training Center. Zeke, who was my earliest distance learning mentor, who provided invaluable insights and experience. He and his staff are without equal in their ability to focus on the learners and use technology as a means to the end and not the end itself.

Karen, my coauthor and colleague. Wow! I have never met someone who so genuinely lives the principles of integrity, customer focus, and quality. Thank you, Karen, for the many memorable hours where sincerity, effort, laughter, and vision combined to produce our book focused on helping others.

and most important, to my wife, Cindy, and my children, Danial, Kari, Bryan, and Kirsten. They sacrificed many hours of "time with Dad" during the writing of the book so that it could be completed. Cindy was my high school sweetheart, became my wife, and if I am fortunate enough, will be my companion forever. Thank you, Cindy, for your eternal love and continuous support.

We both want to thank...

Dr. Susan Fenner, a recognized expert in adult learning, who reviewed every page of the manuscript through the eyes of an ASTD member. Her written comments and recommendations throughout the draft helped us to fine-tune the final copy.

Suzanne Kinkel, for reading the manuscript through the eyes of a trainer, a senior executive of a major corporation, and a visionary thinker.

our friends and colleagues in the distance learning arena who so openly share their knowledge and lessons learned, especially Dr. Chris Olgren, University of Wisconsin; Dr. Phil Westfall, Air Force Institute of Technology; Hank Payne, Federal Aviation Administration; Robbie Smith, Department of Energy; Steve Larkin, Internal Revenue Service; and Lisa Nelson, Environmental Protection Agency.

and special thanks to our friend Ed Kronholm, president of DL Communications, who is a constant source of distance learning news, updates, and guidance.

Karen Mantyla is president of Quiet Power, Inc., a Washington, D.C.-based distance learning training and consulting company. She received her professional certification in distance learning from the University of Wisconsin-Madison, a renowned leader in distance education. Mantyla serves on the board of directors for the Washington Metropolitan Chapter of the United States Distance Learning Association (USDLA) and serves as secretary and active team member for both the technology and communications committees of the Federal Government Distance Learning Association (FGDLA). She is the editor of *Distance Learning News,* the official publication of the Federal Government Distance Learning Association. Mantyla is an active member of the American Society for Training and Development (ASTD) and the Society for Human Resource Management (SHRM). She consults with both public- and private-sector clients to help design, develop, implement, and maintain distance learning systems. Her focus is on the human side of the distance learning equation to ensure that the trainers receive proper support, guidance, and training in selecting and utilizing distance learning methods of delivery. In addition, she helps design learner support systems, tools, and methods to ensure success and continuous process improvement for all remote site facilitators and learners. Mantyla has 15 years of specialized experience in the development and implementation of workplace education programs, with specific emphasis on reaching Learners in dispersed geographic locations. She held many senior leadership positions, including vice president of a Fortune 500 corporation. Karen Mantyla's biography is featured in the 1997 editions of *Who's Who in the World, Who's Who in America, Who's Who of American Women,* and *Who's Who in Finance and Industry*. Her plans include writing and designing additional multimedia resources to help trainers and their organizations achieve distance learning success in the 21st century.

J. Richard "Rick" Gividen is president of Distance Learning Integrators, Inc., a Virginia-based firm specializing in the implementation and continuous improvement of organizational distance learning programs. Distance Learning Integrators offers consulting services, strategic planning assistance, and training workshops designed to enhance organizational distance learning effectiveness. He served for over 15 years in varied training, information management, and leadership positions in the U.S. Army and U.S. Army National Guard (ARNG). His military assignments included distance learning officer, Headquarters, ARNG; chief, Information Management Division, ARNG Professional Education Center; and chairman, Military Science Department, Embry-Riddle Aeronautical University. Gividen earned his B.S. degree in psychology from Brigham Young University. His professional affiliations include the American Society for Training and Development (ASTD); United States Distance Learning Association (USDLA), and the Government Alliance for Training and Education (GATE). Gividen's work with GATE was instrumental in some of the first interagency cooperative distance learning ventures in the federal government. He is married to Cindy Jorgensen Gividen, and they have four children.